Digital Discipline

DIGITAL DISCIPLINE

CHOOSING LIFE IN THE DIGITAL AGE OF EXCESS

HAVARD MELA

NEW YORK

LONDON • NASHVILLE • MELBOURNE • VANCOUVER

Digital Discipline

Choosing Life in the Digital Age of Excess

Published in New York, New York, by Morgan James Publishing. Morgan James is a trademark of Morgan James, LLC. www.MorganJamesPublishing.com

Proudly distributed by Publishers Group West®

Disclaimer: Please note that I do not make any guarantees about the results of the information applied throughout this book. I share educational and informational resources that are intended to help you succeed in managing your technology use. Your ultimate success or failure will be the result of your own efforts, your particular situation, and innumerable other circumstances beyond my knowledge and control.

Morgan James BOGO™

A **FREE** ebook edition is available for you or a friend with the purchase of this print book.

CLEARLY SIGN YOUR NAME ABOVE

Instructions to claim your free ebook edition:
1. Visit MorganJamesBOGO.com
2. Sign your name CLEARLY in the space above
3. Complete the form and submit a photo of this entire page
4. You or your friend can download the ebook to your preferred device

ISBN 9781636982076 paperback
ISBN 9781636982083 ebook
Library of Congress Control Number: 2023936553

Cover Design by:
Rachel Lopez
www.r2cdesign.com

Interior Design by:
Christopher Kirk
www.GFSstudio.com

Morgan James is a proud partner of Habitat for Humanity Peninsula and Greater Williamsburg. Partners in building since 2006.

Get involved today! Visit: www.morgan-james-publishing.com/giving-back

To men and women of any age who seek balance,
emotional freedom, and improved personal relationships
in the digital era of overconsumption.

TABLE OF CONTENTS

INTRODUCTION

*In reading the lives of great men, I found that
the first victory they won was over themselves . . .
self-discipline with all of them came first.*
—Harry S. Truman

This book is written to help free up your time, which is by
far your most precious resource. As our time is limited, it
becomes crucial to discern between activities that bring lasting
happiness and those that drain us. Unfortunately, many of us fall
into the latter category due to excessive time spent online.

Digital Discipline provides the tools to regain control of your
attention, time, and ultimately, your life. It also covers the essential skill of self-discipline, which can enhance your happiness

and effectiveness in all aspects of life. Even though the internet brings tremendous opportunities that our ancestors could only dream of, we often end up devaluing our time on endless distractions. If we want to be more efficient and productive, we must remain in charge of our digital lives. If we can be responsible about our digital use, we can thrive and find real happiness and satisfaction offline.

The purpose of this book is twofold: (1) to help you realize what you want out of life, and (2) to teach you methods of self-discipline, ensuring you reach your goals. Unless you apply self-discipline to your digital habits, you will fall prey to escapism, spending too much time on distractions and entertainment that only sap your energy and provide illusionary fun rather than enduring joy or meaning. By building discipline, you will find the time to pursue what you value the most in life. When you practice and master the habit of self-discipline, you will become more decisive, which will instill confidence, motivation, and clarity regarding your goals. Suddenly, you will know what you want and what you should be spending your time on—or not. It is imperative to be prepared for what life throws your way, and mastering the art of self-discipline is the training that will allow you to get through tough times.

The year 2020 was a perfect example of why it is crucial to set a higher standard for yourself and pave a new, better path to becoming mentally strong. When COVID-19 emerged globally, it threw many people off track because of the unexpected seclusion and free time that was now part of everyone's daily life. Many businesses shut down, leaving their employees with idle, unaccountable hours (some with pay, some without) and no set date in which "normal life" would resume. Many were unprepared to handle the sudden changes that popped up almost daily that year. As a result, many reverted to poor habits and gave in to addictive behaviors—including excessive time spent on their phones and computers. According to a study by the Centers for Disease Control and Prevention (CDC), food insufficiency, loneliness, financial concerns, job loss or fear of job loss, social isolation, and preexisting poor mental health led to people's mental health plummeting in 2020, and people struggled to cope with the uncertainty of how long their lives and careers would be in limbo.[1]

Everyone needs someone close (a friend, partner, or family member) who is mentally tough and can nurture them when they are feeling down. Human nature seeks connection and support, but this inherent desire is often overridden when we self-isolate and spiral into the intangible digital world, where we are mere viewers instead of active, real life participants. Perhaps I'm describing you here? If so, there is no shame. Self-understanding and progress can follow from this point on if you adjust your habits. I'm raising my hand here because I've been in that lonely place, too, where thoughts of real human connection and personal growth were eclipsed by my preference for isolation and traversing the mind-numbing, time-wasting rabbit hole the internet can be.

We don't gain freedom from our undesirable behaviors by going with the flow and taking it easy. We gain freedom by examining certain parts of our lives and setting goals that require discipline. Sometimes we do need to go with the flow and see where the river takes us, but if we use the internet in an unfocused, limitless way, we will waste a lot of time and end up vulnerable to depression and anxiety. Jocko Willink, a former Navy SEAL, titled his best-selling book *Discipline Equals Freedom*, and his words speak volumes to this truth.[2] The discipline that leads to freedom requires taking 100 percent responsibility for yourself and removing as many temptations as possible. Remember, discipline doesn't always mean doing what is *fun*; it means doing what is *required*. What does a new and improved life require of you? *Digital Discipline* will challenge you to push past dispassion and guide you toward daily practices (actionable steps) and rewiring your neural pathways (mental steps).

Social media and passive digital consumption are the cigarettes of our era. We are engaged in an experiment we fail to grasp the full consequences of, and almost everyone is addicted. Some people gradually realize the damaging effects passive digital use has on us. Still, most people are oblivious to the effects, just like most people were oblivious to the harmful effects of cigarettes until the 1960s.

Fundamental changes in society happen without attention to individual differences. Society fails to see the disruptive and harmful impact smartphones and internet addiction have on us. Today's world is filled with abundance, excess, and instant gratification. Yesterday's world revolved around moderation, and it certainly had more limitations on our ability to access data as well as goods and services. (Anyone old enough to have researched school papers with the family's encyclopedia set or at a library?) Until recent years, humans have adapted to living in an environment without stimuli available at our fingertips, and this mismatch gets us into trouble today. Porn, online gambling, online videos, social media, and much more make the digital world abundant today. Therefore, it is up to you to make the necessary changes to avoid the negative consequences of digital addiction.

People use social media for 147 minutes a day, on average.[3] This number accounts for around 10 percent of our daily time, including sleep, but it does not account for the other ways we mismanage time online. We misuse valuable hours passively engaged in online activities that aren't memorable or meaningful. The result is that we end up involving ourselves less in real life experiences. Passive digital use is a pervasive problem among young people, robbing them of youthful enthusiasm and poignant moments they can only experience off-screen.

Growing up, I experienced social anxiety and had difficulties meeting new people. Spending a lot of time online became an easy coping strategy instead of trying to connect with real people in person. While others were partying, I watched porn, movies, or TV series in front of the computer. Whenever I met people, I felt terribly withdrawn and was unable to connect with them. Little did I know that the main reason for my inability to meaningfully connect with others was because of my destructive digital habits.

After experiencing how difficult it felt to interact with others after watching porn or spending a lot of time online, I found a common thread with these behaviors. We feel sluggish and unmotivated if we spend too much time overstimulating ourselves online because doing so gives us constant dopamine spikes. Dopamine is a neurotransmitter that promotes well-being, affects our excitement, and motivates us to action. But if we spend too much time scrolling through TikTok and Instagram, or engaging with video games or porn, our dopamine levels spike temporarily. Yet these behaviors are not able to compel us toward action. In fact, these passive internet passages of time make us *less* compelled to be outward oriented. The ability to self-regulate how much we use our phones and computers is therefore extremely important. We are like rats given constant access to cocaine in one of those experiments. To continue thriving we need discipline and clever strategies to avoid overstimulation. We can't just press the pleasure button without taking some time-outs.

Cultivating digital discipline is a path that will support you in reaching your goals and fulfilling your dreams. Aren't you tired of wasting your life on your digital devices? Have you ever looked back at a week, a month, or a year and wondered where you'd be now in life if you had simply placed limits on scrolling through your phone? If your yearly hours were calculated and presented to you, could you handle the truth of the wasted time? It is a hard hit when you see the truth. I understand that all too well. Actually, you can probably take a guess at how much time a day you are wasting. Then, take that number and add a little more to it . . . that's the real truth. But you can always change your course. That's the beauty of your free will. Determine how you want to refocus your life from this point on. Acceptance is the first step in change. You are not alone in being susceptible to spending too much time online. We are all guilty of this. Don't be upset for too long about your wasted time in the past. But be upset enough to say, "No more!" Then move on to the next step after *examining* and *accepting* what you found—which is *action.* When you're not a slave to your devices, you have the freedom to pursue your life in a focused way and live the life you want. Do your best, be happy with that, and accept that it won't be perfect.

According to the *Collins English Dictionary, self-discipline* is defined as "the ability to control yourself and make yourself work hard and behave in a particular way without needing anyone else to tell you what to do."[4] You could say it is simply overcoming your weaknesses and controlling your feelings. People who reach great success are disciplined; there is no way around it. Discipline is about being able to do what we know we are supposed to, regardless of our short-term emotions. Being disciplined allows us to be efficient and productive, providing a sure path toward reaching our goals. As author Jim Rohn put it: "Discipline is the foundation upon which all success is built. Lack of discipline inevitably leads to failure."[5]

I'm not suggesting that we should stop all digital use. The technology behind our devices makes life more convenient in many ways. For instance, we can still rely on it for work, staying connected, and paying our bills. But there is a way to approach our digital use that ensures we remain in control of it while experiencing its benefits. I call this approach *digital discipline*. Digital discipline allows us to benefit from the positives of digital use and pretty much guarantees that we avoid the negatives. In this book, we define digital use as time spent online on your computer or phone, using apps, watching TV, or playing video games. For example, time spent reading on your Kindle without an internet connection falls outside this definition.

Digital discipline means that we avoid passive digital use and only use our devices for a specific productive or meaningful purpose. For example, if you want to check Facebook, being digitally disciplined would mean having specific things you want to accomplish (checking up on friends, making a post, participating in an educational event, etc.) and completing that task without getting distracted. We will define *passive digital use* as spending more time on a task online or on your digital devices than is necessary to accomplish that task. For example, checking if someone messaged you on FB Messenger or WhatsApp can be okay if planned, but answering the messages and then staying on your phone to browse something else for twenty minutes becomes passive digital use. We should strive to be digitally disciplined and only allow ourselves to finish tasks we have thought of beforehand.

If something seemingly important shows up in your feed, write it down in a notebook or somewhere else and see if it is still important thirty minutes later. It is most likely not critical; it is just your brain tricking you right then and there. That is because the apps and platforms are designed to hack our dopamine system. Remember, dopamine is primarily responsible for motivating us. Interacting with these apps sets off false-positive stimuli that only downregulate our motivation to take action in the real world.

Spending hours clicking on the next recommended video on YouTube is an example of passive use (unless you have a specific goal for watching those videos that will get you closer to the life you want to live). Watching comic videos online can be an example of healthy use if you find it fun and avoid overindulging. Watching a video lecture is also an excellent example of time well spent online. Ultimately, if we spend time online that supports our offline lifestyles, nurtures us, and makes us more capable of handling life's challenges, it is time well spent. That could mean watching a movie occasionally or watching a TV series to get inspired or to relax. But it does not include binge-watching a series until we are half-dead. The moment we realize we are doing something in excess and to the point of numbing out, it is time to put away the phone or computer and do something else.

Sometimes it can be challenging to distinguish between passive and disciplined use. For some people, having a digital dating profile may be beneficial if they use it proactively to reach a specific goal. For others, it can be damaging if they scroll the platform for hours and stare at bikini photos rather than trying to set up dates. We should strive to cut off all digital habits and uses where the drawbacks outweigh the benefits. Much more of our digital use than we think falls into this category. If you answer messages on the phone and end up looking at Instagram posts for an hour, you lost control somewhere in the middle. We will look at strategies to help you avoid wasting time and train you to use digital platforms and social networks so that they only benefit you and don't drain your energy.

Being disciplined with our digital use requires attuning to the present moment to gauge how different digital activities affect us. This cost-benefit analysis is ultimately up to you, and I will provide tools in this book to help you explore your use and decide whether you would like to change some of your digital habits.

Our senses are not entirely objective. Life is multifaceted, and it doesn't care about the confined space between academic disciplines. Therefore, when we look at the issues society and individuals face regarding digital use, we need to look at them from many different perspectives, drawing knowledge from various research fields. I have also done that in this book, using different disciplines to examine the issues with excessive screen time.

Digital Discipline details how to go from a coping lifestyle to a thriving lifestyle, starting with managing your screen time optimally. Discipline in this area is important because like other things in life, we do not know how something affects us fully before it has been around for a long time. For instance, certain prescription drugs that claimed to treat disease and illness were eventually deemed unsafe and taken off the market because of their harmful side effects, which were unknown when first given to patients. Other innovations, too, seemed perfectly safe and harmless in the beginning, yet many years later, severe consequences appeared. Tracing specific side effects to something new can be challenging in the beginning. Screen time might be similar, affecting different people in diverse ways.

We can regain control of our time and attention; it only requires a bit of effort upfront. In the future, I predict that more people will realize the importance of unplugging, and together we can build even more opportunities for meaningful social relationships.

Our attention span is deteriorating, and reading has become more difficult and simply unappealing for many people. We don't think the way we used to. Everything is evaluated for instant gratification and disposability. Real life and its subtleties don't do it for us anymore because the online apps and websites have built-in features to capture our attention and "game" our dopamine systems.

Our relationships with others are perhaps the most important aspect of our lives. We are wired to connect with others, yet we face a big issue today with too much screen time, disrupting our communication patterns. When we do have meaningful interactive experiences with others, we feel fulfilled and happy because the brain releases neurotransmitters that make us feel good. Sadly, a lot of our in-person social time is being replaced with messages, social media posts, and other digital alternatives. We do not connect as deeply when we use digital replacements compared to meeting people in person. As a result, we are undermining our foundation for happiness.

Real life doesn't offer as easy or frequent rewards as we can get online. In real life, patience and hard work are necessary to become successful. Getting the replica online requires no effort. Therefore, some people will stay at home and use the internet to fuel a cycle of endless, easy pleasure. This does not have to be you. It is possible to turn any situation around by taking some proactive steps! This book is for anyone interested in living a better life, starting with cultivating digital discipline. Having digital discipline might very well be the most critical factor to all of us living in the attention economy—the digital economy in which everyone is competing for our attention. In this economy, the product is our time spent engaging with content since it drives ad revenue; as a result, our sustained attention becomes scarce and therefore valuable. To avoid becoming passive consumers of digital use in the attention economy, we must transition into proactive users.

When we look at our smartphones instead of the people around us, it kills the possibility of spontaneous conversations in the elevator or in the line at the coffee shop. These small conversations are surprisingly crucial for our well-being. They are neglected due to a shifting awareness during that moment. We forget to take a deep breath and look around. We no longer smile at that attractive stranger or engage in small talk in the Starbucks line since our focus is elsewhere.

With the number of potential pitfalls in the digital world, some contrarianism is required. Most people don't apply discipline to their digital use. To avoid the negative effects of too much digital use, you need to develop the ability to withstand social pressure. Without it, you will go with the masses, whose behavior doesn't account for personal differences. You need to build independence and the ability to follow your vision. Do this, and you will be well-rewarded with inner peace and strength.

If you can build your self-control to a level where you only use your devices consciously, you will have more time on your hands and the earned discipline to accomplish other things. The playing field is not even fair anymore. If you control your attention and digital use, you will have a considerable edge, regardless of your pursuit. Following the steps in this book will give you back several hours of your day. They will feel like a gift, and you will want to safeguard this newfound time with life-enhancing activities.

The internet is a fantastic resource, but only if we are conscious about our use. In the first part of the book, we will go deeper into how the brain works and how it is exploited by technology. We will then explore how we operate socially and understand how the notion of happiness works. You will also gain an understanding of why digital discipline is necessary to thrive in today's world, which will prompt you to modify your behavior. Moving forward with new tools at your disposal, you can then choose to live your life pretty much how you want—enjoying the freedoms and rewards of your set intentions.

In part 2, you will see how you can implement behavioral change into your life. The most important thing is building discipline since this is the foundation for everything. It goes deeper than adopting mere techniques and habits. This book is ultimately about living your life the way you want. Together, we will build the strength to avoid unnecessary temptations and distractions. Life in the twenty-first century calls for this ability.

The objective of this book is *not* to tell you how you should live your life; instead, it aims to plant some ideas. The focus is mostly on overarching principles and concepts rather than strict rules and techniques. The world is changing rapidly, and we must be in touch with society. Therefore, if people spend increasing amounts of time online in the future, we need to consider the benefits and drawbacks, then decide on (based on our unique life circumstances) the best course of action. The best course of action will be different for each person. Hopefully, this book can provide the tools you need to make an informed decision for yourself and demonstrate how you can best navigate the attention economy.

At the end of every chapter, I have included some exercises to help you become more conscious of your digital habits. When you realize how your unconscious digital habits affect you, it will be easier to change them—and to know why changing them is important. Later in the book, I will detail how you can cultivate digital discipline and, ultimately, a better life.

This book is essentially about not always doing what is easy but rather what is right. As you read, avoid checking your phone regardless of how much you want to. Make that promise to yourself. This will be the first of many small battles on your way to cultivating digital discipline.

Changing your digital habits out of the blue is not easy. You need to build resilience to take conscious control of how and when you use screens, and in this book, you will learn how. Life is beautiful on the other side. Real joy and excitement will follow when you consciously manage your digital use.

PART 1

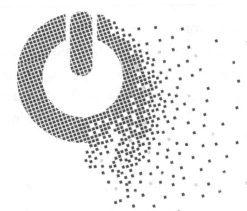

CHAPTER I

WHERE IS TECHNOLOGY TAKING US?

*The difference between technology and slavery is that
slaves are fully aware that they are not free.*
—Nassim Nicholas Taleb

We live in perhaps the greatest time in history. If we manage to use the tools at our disposal the right way, we can live incredible lives. Discipline is the key. Know what you want, go for it, and avoid distractions. This chapter aims to wake you up and help you gain awareness as to why you need to change your digital habits.

Here are some of the many side effects of digital overuse that signal you should change your digital habits. Other problems can cause some of these side effects, but you will know if these speak to your digital overuse or not. If you are familiar with any of these side effects, you should become more conscious of how you spend your time online.

- You associate your phone with stress.
- You have trouble sleeping and use devices right before you go to bed.
- You are incapable of not checking your phone when you experience a couple of minutes of boredom.
- You frequently get lost in certain apps or end up spending too much time online, then wake up from a trance minutes or hours later.
- You don't feel the same joy you previously did from other activities, such as hanging out with friends.
- You don't have time for important projects at school or work because you procrastinate by spending time online.

There is an epidemic of disconnection and loneliness. Unfortunately, the more connected we get online, the more disconnected we get from real life. Many people favor texting over conversations on the phone. We are becoming more self-absorbed and connect in more shallow ways than we used to. It is much easier to scroll on social media for an hour or two in the evening than to meet up with some friends. Convenience is, in many ways, our worst enemy. We tend to choose the path of least resistance.

Many former executives and high-level employees are beginning to speak out against social media. Chris Hughes, a cofounder of Facebook, has said that it is time for Facebook to be broken up and regulated.[6] Brian Acton, the founder of WhatsApp, tweeted "#deletefacebook" in 2018.[7] And Tristan Harris, a cofounder of the Center for Humane Technology, discussed social platforms' dangers in the documentary *The Social Dilemma.*

Tristan Harris is an outspoken critic of social media and how digital platforms capture our attention. He founded the startup Apture, which Google acquired in 2011. Harris then spent a few years working at Google as a design ethicist before deciding he had seen enough. He shared a lengthy and hugely popular presentation about the responsibility Google employees should feel for how the platform's users spend their time. Tristan believes that the human mind can be hijacked and that we involuntarily spend our time on smartphones only to be disempowered. He is also very worried about the race to capture our attention, especially the attention of kids.[8]

It is quite telling that tech-free schools, such as the Waldorf School of Peninsula in the heart of Silicon Valley, are filled with tech employees' children.[9]

People are worth more to tech companies if they are confused, overstimulated, and uncertain than if they are thriving and living great lives. Social media companies are incentivized to make us spend as much time as possible on their platforms since ads are how they capitalize on users. For example, kids often have no other choice than to use certain tech platforms to stay in touch with their friends. If kids lived the way they used to before PlayStation and computers, they wouldn't have time to consume content for hours online and would instead choose to go outdoors and have adventures rather than stay at home. This is the big problem with tech companies' business models; they are incentivized to make us miserable and spend time in front of screens instead of us being actively and intentionally engaged in our lives. They essentially hack our reward system to make a profit.

Our reward system is a group of structures in the brain responsible for fueling our desire to reach rewards, like food, money or sex. In this book, you will encounter the words *sensitization* and *desensitization*. Sensitizing your brain means that you become more sensitive to pleasure, and desensitization makes you less capable of feeling pleasure. If we build a healthy approach to digital use and avoid overstimulation, we will become more sensitive to pleasure in other areas of life!

You are more sensitive to dopamine if you have a sensitized dopamine system. That means you will feel the positive effects when it is released strongly or you release more dopamine from the same activity than if you have overstimulated your dopamine system. When we become more sensitive to rewards, we become more willing to work hard to reach our goals. On the other hand, if we have a desensitized reward system, we will be more prone to apathy and less willing to do what is necessary to achieve what we want.

If we cannot get the intimacy or closeness we need from our relationships, it is easy to fill the void with distractions online. I can think of numerous examples from my life when I felt lonely and thus distracted myself online to avoid painful feelings. The result was that it became more difficult for me to connect with others. My escape into the digital world fueled a downward spiral that made things worse.

Feeling lonely from time to time is actually healthy. Uncomfortable emotions are the best motivators for change. If you feel a bit lonely, you will probably do something to connect with more people and build a bigger peer group. By constantly distracting ourselves with screen time, we avoid feeling those uncomfortable feelings that could have made us grow.

We can access anything we want online at any time. You can get sexually aroused in seconds by a photo or video you can pull up—for free! If you want to get inspired to become more powerful, you can watch a James Bond movie. But that's where it ends. Inspiration does not equate to action in many cases, especially when using digital media as a crutch for apathy or boredom. In our ancestors' hunter-gatherer days, looking around the savanna or the forest for food and danger was crucial for survival. Nowadays, googling various topics you are curious about partly hijacks our ancestral instincts.

Facebook's stated purpose is to connect us. Oh, the irony. Many of the apps we use to communicate with people make us lonelier instead. We spend more time "connecting" with people online at the expense of meeting up in real life. If we only use these platforms to facilitate meetings, they can help us in some meaningful ways. It is when we spend time consuming content passively that we get into trouble.

Internet addiction can be defined as compulsive internet use that has a significant negative impact on other areas of life over time.[10] If we fail to be social enough, distracting ourselves online becomes an easy coping strategy. I decided to build better digital habits in 2019. Before that, I had a limited social circle and spent most of my spare time online on YouTube, watching TV, and passively using social media. My internet addiction had made me emotionally numb and unable to connect with people.

When I decided to change this, I first experienced some long evenings by myself reading books. After a while, I started feeling lonely. The strange thing was that I hadn't felt lonely before, even though I had spent just as much time alone. Distractions and numbing myself probably made the feeling go away temporarily. Loneliness was a great motivator, and it made me seek out connections with more people. Eventually, I got more friends and a better social life, and I didn't have to spend the evenings after work or university by myself anymore. A new world opens up when we get to the other side and find replacements for passive digital use. Then, we can experience life filled with activities that excite us. From time to time, I fell back into old, mindless, unproductive routines and watched YouTube for hours. Every time I did that, I didn't feel the same drive to be social in the aftermath. This piqued my curiosity about neuroscience and how screen time affects us. I started to think that distracting ourselves online affects our ability to connect with other people.

When I started to reduce my screen time significantly, massive changes happened. Some of them were surprising. I felt capable of reading subtle nuances of social interactions much better than I had earlier. For example, I could read facial expressions more accurately and felt confident holding eye contact with people. I became more social and started feeling real pleasure from connecting with people again. I simply became a more outgoing person by avoiding excessive digital use. After this, I started hypothesizing that engaging with a lot of stimulating content online, like watching porn, downregulates our neurotransmitters, making us less capable of connection and less engaged in our lives. This sparked my interest in researching the effects technology has on us.

When we use social media, for example, by scrolling through TikTok feeds, we get a short-lived dopamine surge. This feels good, and the dopamine spike entices us to continue. That is why we look for the next video or the next picture. An hour later, when we feel numbed out, our dopamine levels have fallen below the baseline, and it takes a while before they get back up. That is why we tend to feel sluggish after passive digital use. If we get a big deviation upward of dopamine, the brain will try to reach equilibrium by pushing dopamine below the baseline in the aftermath.

Here are some of the benefits of cultivating digital discipline and being more conscious about how we use technology:

- Sleep patterns improve, providing rest and healing to the brain and body
- Perspective broadens because of the extra time to focus on other things
- Activity levels increase, positively impacting your physical health
- Mental health improves, creating a more positive mindset
- Productivity increases, improving your career and personal life

PAIN AND PLEASURE

In the Western world, we have access to endless pleasure and get exposed to minimal pain or struggle in our daily lives. You might disagree, thinking that pain is everywhere! We get sick, endure breakups, lose our jobs, and get into disagreements with our friends and family. True, but I'm comparing the average modern-day life to a life from one hundred years ago and then going back farther in time. We can take the bus to work or drive. We can avoid being outside when it rains. We do not have to grow and find our food or store supplies for the off-season. We have access to prime medical care, and we certainly have more purchasing options for clothing, makeup, entertainment, and travel. Smartphones can bring us instant pleasure, and most office jobs are sedentary. This leads to constant exposure to pleasurable situations and not enough pain.

The reason why we need pain is that the body is always trying to achieve equilibrium—a state of balance. A runner's high is so sought after because it produces chemicals that a day in the office cannot. After experiencing something challenging like intense workouts, the body rewards us with feel-good hormones. When we constantly get exposed to pleasure, we don't get the chance to release the same feel-good neurochemicals to counteract pain. If you do a cold plunge, your dopamine levels will be elevated for hours, yet they won't fall below the baseline afterward. On the other hand, if you stare at bikini photos on Instagram, you only end up with short-lived dopamine spikes before dipping below your baseline dopamine levels very quickly.

Pain toughens us mentally and makes the body adjust by providing endorphins and other feel-good chemicals to counteract the pain. We are meant to be active for hours every day. We were not meant to sit in front of a screen, pressing on a pleasure-lever (as we do when we scroll through pictures of Instagram models). Our brains have adjusted throughout evolution not to get flooded with easy dopamine but rather to derive subtle pleasure from hard work and the fruits of labor. Think about it: Our ancestors thousands of years ago had to hunt for food, gather resources, and constantly work just to survive. That gave them more pain than we experience nowadays. But that also gave the body the chance to compensate by releasing endorphins while running for hours and having rushes of adrenaline. Technology is moving faster nowadays than our bodies and minds can change.

RISK VS. CHALLENGE

We need a bit of discomfort and multiple challenges daily to thrive. This seems counterintuitive. But if we go too long without challenges, the body doesn't get the chance to release feel-good chemicals to compensate for pain. That is why we need to exercise, be active in our daily tasks, and mentally challenge ourselves on a regular basis. When we push back against the life of ease that calls to us like a siren song, we find that we take more risks (not life-threatening risks but productive ones relating to our career, social life, physical endurance, etc.). Exposing ourselves to daily challenges helps us remain positive and mentally strong.

What is the difference between a *risk* and a *challenge*? A challenge is something that we know might pull us out of our comfort zone and require effort we don't feel up to when we are in a spiral of isolation, addiction, and low energy. A risk is something we have to think twice about doing because if done hastily, it can be detrimental. But that is not to say risk is negative. On the contrary! Calculated risks that pan out provide the excitement we need. For instance, both risks and challenges require us to face our fears and generate an outcome that either works in our favor or not. One comes with higher stakes (risk); the other generally holds lower stakes (challenge). You benefit from both in your life!

When everything is too easy, we can start to get negative and worry about small, petty things. We need something to overcome! We were built this way. If a few obstacles or hard-earned successes don't show up, we need to find a way to experience a bit of discomfort by taking on new routines, such as taking a cold shower every morning. Replacing some pleasure-inducing activities with tougher challenges can actually make us happier. Start going for a run instead of zoning out to Netflix. Meditate instead of mindlessly browsing through social media. The body is extremely good at adapting, and when we lean toward the side of pain and discomfort, the body compensates us handsomely. Please don't overdo it, of course; I am not advocating self-harm of any kind, but some challenges and risks will only do us good.

We will all experience a bit of pain every day, no matter what. Stop running away from the opportunity to grow. Accept the discomfort, then navigate your way through and see how you become stronger, gain knowledge, or come out better in some way. If you decide to watch a movie and eat potato chips instead of going for a run, it will be pleasurable right then and there, but you will pay for it with your long-term happiness. Pain will only appear in a different, greater form later in your life if you constantly go for the easiest option. It will also show up as diminished self-esteem in the short-term. Avoiding discomfort is perhaps the easiest way to ruin your life. As a teenager, I was very shy and would opt out of social situations when they made me uncomfortable. That only worsened my shyness, making it impossible for me to have a girlfriend, for example. Eventually, I had to start pushing myself, but I should have done it sooner. The only thing that would have happened if I had remained unsocial is that I would have ended up living a life of isolation much more painful than a few awkward moments here and there interacting with new friends.

NEUROTRANSMITTERS AND SUPERNORMAL STIMULI

Neurotransmitters in the brain significantly affect how we feel. When neural circuits are used to fuel addiction, dopamine and other neurotransmitters are released. That makes us feel good. If we follow an addiction, dopamine production will be down-regulated and dopamine receptors will be reduced, meaning we become less sensitive to pleasurable experiences if we follow our addictions.[11] Think about that for a second. And let's face it. There is no doubt that most of us are addicted to our smartphones, which affects the pleasure we derive from other things. That means we find it harder to get motivated by or derive pleasure from the small things in life, such as going out of the house to watch the sunset or hiking to see your favorite view.

Nobel Prize–winning scientist Nikolaas Tinbergen came up with the concept of "'supernormal stimuli,' a phenomenon wherein artificial stimuli can be created that will override an evolutionarily developed genetic response."[12] Supernormal stimuli are artificial alternatives to natural reward responses.[13] A good example is watching porn, which is an exaggerated version of having sex—not necessarily better but sometimes more visual. Junk food, packed with sugar and fats, is also an example of something we never would have encountered before this age of technology, and it is made to exploit how much we like calorie-dense foods. Perhaps the most harmful supernormal stimuli are the drugs that mimic natural pleasure and reduce our capacity to feel the same joy later naturally, such as cocaine and ecstasy. Every time we eat junk food or watch porn, we create or strengthen new neural pathways for pleasure at the expense of the natural ones. The result is that we become desensitized to natural, whole foods or natural sexual attraction.

Evolutionarily, we are wired to grip opportunities to experience rewards. As a result, we can easily binge on high-fat food or end up scrolling through sexy images online. The only thing that stops us from doing so is our prefrontal cortex, which controls our willpower. The internet provides infinite artificial stimuli, and our natural inclination and curiosity to explore could be weakened as a result. We have neural pathways that fire every time we engage in certain behaviors. Every time we scroll mindlessly on social media platforms, we become more inclined to scroll online when bored instead of going out in the world and actually doing something. When we engage in these unconscious digital habits, we find less excitement and happiness in the real world. If you are bored, isn't it better to start going outside to meet people, reading, or going for a run than to start scrolling? Unfortunately, every time we take that easy way out, we also make it easier to do the same in the future.

If you constantly watch porn or other intensely stimulating things online, playing the guitar will seem dull by comparison. In order to enjoy playing board games with your family or get lost reading a good book, you'll have to avoid constant dopamine spikes from your phone. You can use the smartphone, of course, but be conscious and take breaks throughout the day.

Many people cannot resist looking at their cell phones when they are alone. It can even be painful for some people when the constant buzz of stimuli from screens is removed. A few years back, simple activities like cooking dinner were very uncomfortable for me because I constantly stimulated myself with movies, TV series, or porn. Now, I enjoy cooking since I have been accustomed to the subtler pace of real life. We can find greater joy in the small things life offers, such as a swim on a warm summer day, if we avoid overstimulating ourselves online.

Our capacity to feel pleasure is closely linked to how sensitized our brains are. You can sensitize your dopamine system by being conscious of the stimuli you expose yourself to. Limit your consumption of activities that spike your dopamine a lot, such as watching porn, spending a lot of time on social media, taking drugs, eating junk food, and so on. The result is that you will become more easily excited and derive more pleasure from simpler things. Our inner peace is easily affected by our constant search for distractions. Inner peace is the foundation for both happiness and excellent work. We need to find peace within ourselves to thrive, and in the twenty-first century it is more important than ever. Remaining in control of our attention is difficult but sorely needed. The alternative is being at the whim of our environment and following the path of least resistance. It is very easy to fill our impulsive need for stimuli and distractions. If you are not careful, years can go by where you get trapped in a daze, and you realize you've missed out on the valuable experiences only real life offers.

DISTRACTIONS AND OTHER DANGERS WITH DIGITAL OVERUSE

It is easy to reach for our phones when we have nothing to do. Finding someone who isn't on their phone while riding on the bus or metro is challenging. Take a look next time! I'll bet nearly everyone gets on their phone at some point on the ride. Very few pay attention to their environment on their commute since the smartphone is more stimulating. *What is the problem with using the phone when you are on the metro?* you might be thinking. Maybe you don't know what you feel, only that you feel an urge. You might think it is a good chance to answer people or check something you've been meaning to check. Of course, it can be an excellent opportunity to do tasks and answer messages.

The point is not that you should avoid the phone at all costs. The point is to get used to gazing around the environment and feeling good without any stimuli. Resisting the *impulse* to check shows discipline and denying the *urge* to check shows self-control. Give yourself a specific time frame to look at your phone on the metro, for example, then tune in to real life around you. We experience less solitude and time without intense stimuli when we have constant access to digital stimuli. Therefore, it is very important sometimes to have some time alone—time that is akin to meditation.

Often, when we decide to check our notifications or check our phones as if we are on autopilot, we are really trying to avoid boredom. Other times, we use it as an avoidance tool to avoid diving deeply into negative feelings and facing discomfort. I find that if I am sleep deprived or otherwise having a bad day, it is much easier to start scrolling mindlessly on social media or watch videos passively for hours than if I am energized and refreshed. In these circumstances, it is essential to be disciplined. I remember plenty of times that I almost felt like a zombie after spending too much time online, looking for the next form of digital entertainment. It could start with YouTube or reading the news, and I would gradually need something more stimulating.

When we are tired, it is much easier for our unhealthy, unhealed lower self to emerge. It is not difficult for this negative part of your psyche to have a "no limitations" party online. Common ways of doing this include looking up controversial content that you know will stimulate your temper, making negative comments online (don't be that person!), comparing yourself to others and feeling like you fall short, and making large purchases you can't afford.

There are many fantastic online tools for entertainment, connecting with people, learning, and much more. YouTube has an endless digital archive. Social media has enabled people to connect online and made it easier for people to stay in touch. We can also google anything we can think of. The internet has made life much more convenient for us, no doubt about it. If we could learn to use the internet in a *disciplined* way to seek out new information instead of allowing the mindless, brain-damaging hours to continue, we would be much better off. This happens because the most used tools online have a "drug" component to them. Facebook enables us to stay in touch with people but also distracts us and exposes us to content meant to capture our attention. All the most used online platforms have a tool component and a drug component. To overcome the drug component, we need discipline.

How often have you checked your email or paid a bill and gotten sucked into something else? Suddenly, you receive a notification, and before you know it, you have wasted two hours scrolling through Instagram pictures, thinking about what the hell happened to the time. Our phones and all the apps we've downloaded can get us into a dopamine-seeking loop where our brains pretty much turn into mush. Dopamine is associated with desire and looking for rewards such as food. When we scroll online, our brains can get caught up in dopamine loops where they want more and more stimuli. This weakness in our reward system is taken advantage of by almost everything we do on smartphones. If we get into a dopamine-seeking loop, hours can go by before we awaken from the digitally induced trance. The problem with this behavior is that it can desensitize our dopamine system, making us less motivated and interested in other rewarding experiences.

On social media platforms, the brain's primal tendencies are exploited fully at every turn. When you get into a dopamine loop, you look for the next thing that can renew your interest and click on the next video without thinking. Then, your brain will look for the next source of dopamine when the previous one is exhausted. The same happens when we click on the next porn scene. The exact mechanism that would make us go to the hilltop to search for food now makes us log on to social networks and browse through pictures in a perpetual cycle to feed our social or other cravings.

Almost everything in our environment is meant to lure us into experiencing instant dopamine hits. We can eat junk food, check social media, watch videos online, go out for drinks, look at arousing photos, or do several other things to experience instant stimuli. That is how most people live. Our baseline dopamine levels fall, and our endurance, self-discipline, work ethic, and focus suffer as a result. We lose passion and zest to go for our highest aspirations every time we follow our impulses to gain instant pleasure online.

I remember periods of my life in my early twenties when I had no motivation whatsoever. I had no motivation to be social, find a girlfriend, go to university, or do anything with my life because my terrible digital habits desensitized my dopamine system, inhibiting the motivation I needed to make something of myself. My motivation returned after I developed digital discipline and avoided these bad habits. I will not pretend it was easy to cultivate digital discipline, but later in the book, you will discover how you can do it too.

REINFORCEMENT AND DESENSITIZATION

Our brains are flexible, which means they are malleable and can be changed. This concept is known as neuroplasticity. With every action or inaction, we either reinforce or weaken specific pathways in our brain. Every time we log on to social media, we strengthen specific neural pathways. Most of the widely used social platforms online are just giant conditioning stations. Dopamine fluctuations are excellent at programming us to avoid or engage in certain behaviors. Psychologist B. F. Skinner showed that we learn through reinforcement when dopamine is involved.[14] The best way to condition someone to do something is to provide variable rewards. A slot machine is a perfect example of this. It doesn't give you a payout every time, but it could be the next spin that gives you the payout, which is why slot machines are so addictive.

There is a significant discrepancy between how easy it is to release dopamine online and the effort required to secure rewards in real life. In real life, there is a much bigger delay from taking action to experiencing the reward. Online, we can have the pleasure immediately. This mismatch makes us less willing to work for what we want in life. Think about it. Have you noticed that watching a movie in the morning can affect your motivation for the rest of your day? I certainly feel this. If I wake up and use my phone too much in the morning, I will lose motivation to accomplish my daily goals. Why? Because I have already released dopamine from scrolling on the phone. Then, going out there in the world to hustle will seem more pointless because I have already experienced the dopamine I would get from working toward and achieving my goals. Dopamine is what gives us the energy to work toward our goals. That is why passive digital use is our number one enemy.

I wish everybody had a sensitive dopamine system. If you are desensitized, everything feels heavy, and nothing can make you excited. I used to feel that way. Now I get excited and have fun constantly. The difference is how sensitive we are to the pleasure associated with dopamine and its effect on motivation. You will work harder, have more fun, be more excited, and gain a more positive outlook if you sensitize your dopamine system. In addition, you will be a more positive influence on the people around you.

Many people have behavioral addictions these days. To modify our behavior, we may have to remove triggers. I am careful with certain movies, Instagram, and a few other things to avoid being triggered to watch porn. Others have to avoid triggers for gambling or smoking pot, for example. It is typical to be exposed to triggers online for things we want to avoid or spend less time on. We need to be mindful of this in our daily digital lives so we can build new, alternative neural pathways and avoid triggering ones that could take us down routes we don't want to go.

STAYING CONNECTED

If you become digitally disciplined and begin reading instead of watching a TV series for hours or stop scrolling Instagram endlessly, there will be consequences. Some of the people you have been communicating with primarily online might stop chatting with you as much, so you may drift away from them. Such platonic relationships might be weakened, but that is a small price to pay. If you free up hours every day, you suddenly have a significant advantage over others, regardless of what you want to do, and a lot more energy and time.

Every time we do something or say yes to something, another door closes simultaneously. We can't be everything at once. There will also be drawbacks if you decide to stop using social networks altogether. For example, setting up get-togethers on social media is common, so you may lose out on some of these opportunities if you don't have a digital presence. With a disciplined approach, you can have a digital presence but avoid getting hijacked by social platforms such as Facebook and Snapchat. It can be wise to choose just a few platforms rather than have all of them. For example, if you have Instagram, Facebook, and WhatsApp, you might not need TikTok and Snapchat. Reflect on whether you could remove some social networks from your life without any consequences. Most of us could remove a few and be much better off.

Many people think they will lose out on various activities and fun if they stop spending so much time on social networks. Their friends use it all the time, so they are afraid of being left out. True, we might lose out on some things, but better opportunities await us if we cultivate digital discipline. Remember, digital discipline means that we use the smartphone as long as it aids our lives; we stop using it as soon as it affects us negatively. If you are moving to a new country to study abroad, for instance, it can be nice to have social media to find events, join group chats with classmates, and so on. But we should still not spend more time on social networks than necessary. Some people can get away with not using social media altogether. But the sustainable approach for most of us is to use some social media apps only to stay in touch with people and build discipline and awareness to avoid passive use.

Experiment and see what happens if you spend less time on social media. Most likely, you will not lose out on much since people will call or text you if it is something important or if they want to meet up with you. When we stop compulsive digital use, we soon see new opportunities, socially and in other ways. I became much more social when I cut down on screen time, which radically strengthened my relationships. The same can happen to you.

DIGITAL USE, SOCIAL RELATIONSHIPS, AND COMMON ISSUES

We are an incredibly social species. The human need for connection is powerful and has a massive impact on our health. Our relationships are often considered the most crucial aspect of our lives. Strong social bonds strengthen our mental and physical health. Having good relationships has been proven to make us live longer. On the contrary, the social isolation of healthy people ruins them psychologically and sometimes even physically.

Generation Z (born between 1997 and 2012) is on the verge of a mental health crisis. Weaker relationships because of too much screen time is a substantial contributing factor. We spend less time with people, and our time being social tends to get disrupted by our smartphones. We even have a new word for ignoring someone in favor of our phone, called "phubbing."[15] The result is that we spend less time connecting, and when we do, we connect in a shallower way.

A Gallup Poll revealed that people viewed their relationships with their families and health as the most important parts of their lives. Family relationships came out on top, even above health. The other relationships we have with our coworkers, friends, and acquaintances are also significant.[16] You don't have to be a rocket scientist to realize that our digitalized lifestyles negatively impact our relationships. It is more difficult to bond with others because of the competing influence of the screen.

As humans, we have the capacity to think about the meaning of life. That is why feeling a sense of connection and belonging is so important. We also know the vastness of time and space at a deep, spiritual level. It makes us feel like there is a point to existing and that our time on Earth matters when we are connected to other people.

Just like drug addicts are usually the last ones to admit they have a problem, very few people have the necessary distance from the pervasive issue of spending time on digital distractions to realize how negatively it affects us. In addition, the human psyche is excellent at explaining its behavior as rational. There is even a cognitive bias called *commitment and consistency* tendency, which demonstrates that people will continue doing what they have done in the past because they don't want to go against their own identity.[17] We seldom question our ingrained habits, such as checking social media perpetually.

There is a mass psychosis with how we use our smartphones and spend time online. Since it is the norm, there is no sane majority to point out the problem. I can assure you of the benefits of being digitally disciplined. It is almost like you get younger. You gain years back. You get more energy, and your mind feels clearer. You feel more alive. The sedating effect of too much screen time (in particular, passive screen time) is alarming.

Tiny habits compound, for better or worse. Deciding to be more disciplined with your digital habits might not seem like a big deal, but a few years later, it could have snowballed into something much bigger. When we remove activities that sap our energy, we start a positive momentum that has the potential to continue perpetually. For me, this meant starting a business on the side while earning my degree, building my social network, and having the time to write.

Our minds need time to sort out all the information we encounter in solitude. Try to become aware of how you feel the next time you spend time passively online. Do you feel uncentered and experience racing thoughts? It is by becoming aware that we can make changes. Try to habitually pay attention to the signals your body tells you about passive digital use. Pretty soon, you will probably be able to tell the subtle way it affects your energy. From that point, you can choose habits that make your life better.

GETTING TO KNOW YOURSELF

Many people lack a sense of purpose and direction due to endless distractions. Sometimes, you must allow yourself to feel negative emotions like loneliness, anger, and boredom. Negative emotions and frustration can be viewed as a signal to make a change. If we suppress the slightest hint of boredom or sadness with digital entertainment, we numb ourselves from the frustration that could have caused us to step up and take action. Obviously, it can be time well spent to watch a good series or movie, but consuming content for hours every day has a steep cost.

We experience frustration when we don't have what we want. If you want a girlfriend or boyfriend, you can reduce the slight frustration temporarily by watching porn. This pleasure will destroy your natural motivation to get what you want. In many ways, frustration is the best motivation there is. You do not step up because everything is perfect already. You step up because you know you could do much better, and frustration is the key to unlocking that motivation.

ARE SOCIAL NETWORKS CONSUMER-FRIENDLY?

In *A New Earth*, Eckhart Tolle explains that watching television may temporarily turn off thinking, allowing us to relax. It is only temporary; afterward, we tend to ruminate on thoughts induced by the shows we have watched. Tolle particularly warns about watching a TV series where the images change very rapidly. *A New Earth* was published in 2005, so we can only imagine what he would have said about TikTok, Instagram, YouTube, and Snapchat, for example. Eckhart explains that spiritual growth involves becoming less focused on our thoughts and instead becoming present, simply observing our surroundings without labeling them. Try to notice how much you identify with your thoughts the next time you spend time online unconsciously. Do you manage to turn off your thoughts and be present? Does it become easier to be present when you have more disciplined digital habits? Try to become aware of these patterns in your daily life. Life is optimal when we are fully present in whatever we do, and Eckhart says that it is only in *presence* that we can do great work.[18]

The big tech companies don't hire just anyone to design features that get our attention. They employ some of the most brilliant people in the world, graduates from MIT, Stanford, and other prestigious schools. Having studied neuroscience, computer science, behavioral psychology, or other similar fields for years, they understand precisely how to exploit the weaknesses that lie within your brain. The main problem with social networks such as Instagram is that the incentives are misaligned with the common good. Time spent away from our lives being distracted and desensitized is good for Meta Platforms, the parent company of WhatsApp, Facebook, and Instagram. Ad revenue is what drives the attention economy. It has reached a point where the average American checks their phone ninety-six times a day![19] Don't tell me you receive ninety-six urgent messages daily. Hopefully, more people will wake up to the problems social networks and their business models bring. When enough people begin to take this seriously, we can enforce change that will help us protect our attention. Long-term, things might get better. But for now, we need to take the individual approach and make sure we consciously control our attention.

One of the ways big tech is so great at hacking our brains is by embedding certain features and algorithms into social platforms. The Like button exploits our need for approval, and it has been remarkably effective at making us spend more time online. Facebook's feed exposes us to something new every time we refresh it. And every time you leave YouTube, TikTok, or another social media app, the self-learning algorithm becomes a bit more accurate at predicting how to make you stay longer next time. Some of the most profitable businesses globally are spending their capital on building even greater algorithms to make us spend even more time on useless activities online. The result is that ordinary people miss out on life to a bigger and bigger degree.

Many digital platforms have developed algorithms that can read our emotional states with surprising accuracy. The algorithms analyze what kind of stimuli we respond most strongly to and what kinds of emotional states we inhabit. The information is exploited to generate revenue. Based on this, products are recommended at the "perfect timing." YouTube, Netflix, and TikTok, among others, have designed their platforms to take advantage of our inherent laziness. When we are finished with a video or episode, a new one will begin unless we interfere.

RECOMMENDATION MEDIA: A NEW MODEL

In the future, many platforms will likely make synthetic media to create the perfect content that suits your needs at any given time. Imagine this scenario: You log on to one of your favorite apps, and as you start scrolling, a video with precisely the content that hits your emotional state the best starts playing (all made from AI). Then as your mood changes (which the algorithm can read based on how fast you scroll, among other things), different videos will be shown to capture your attention for as long as possible. Much of the content might not even be real—it's simply synthetic media created just for you to stimulate you as much as possible. We might not be too far away from a future like this.

TikTok popularized content based on our preferences with algorithmic content distribution. Now other digital platforms have started favoring preference-based content rather than showing you what you follow as well. Facebook has partly done this, which is the direction social media is moving in. When scrolling through your feed, you might see videos of complete strangers rather than your friend's new photo because the algorithm found it more emotionally relevant to you. The result is that you might miss out on an important update in your life. Because of this, we need to be conscious of the benefits of various networks compared with the downsides. It is time to log off and go more old school again. Purer social networks without all the irrelevant updates, such as BeReal, might be the best bet to connect with friends. Or even better, pick up the phone to call them instead!

MY STORY

A few years ago, I couldn't read an article online without losing focus. My attention span and concentration ability were so weak that it was practically impossible for me to read a book. I had little power and control over my life. At times, I felt helpless. My social skills and sociability were greatly affected. It was when I decided to build discipline that my life changed. The first change I made was not to use the internet after ten o'clock at night. In this period of my life, I went to university and had very irregular sleeping patterns. At times, I would be awake for several hours, and the only thing I had to fill the hours was books. After a while, I started to notice some benefits. I began to feel more centered and calmer. And, as I mentioned earlier, it felt more natural to communicate with other people.

Communicating and being around other people is supposed to feel natural and effortless. It had never felt that way until that point in my life, when I finally avoided the continuous dopamine hits from spending time on my smartphone and computer. I had to recognize that I had become reliant on them. For the first time in my adult life, I avoided overstimulating myself, and the result was that other things could stimulate me. In the beginning, it was difficult to put the phone away, which was actually great because it cultivated discipline. That newfound discipline allowed me to accomplish things like reading, studying better, and being active, and spending time with friends felt more natural.

We are becoming emotionally numb these days, and the numbness only intensifies. We are meant to feel joy and pleasure from certain activities that "don't do it for us" anymore. Adults who grew up in the era before smartphones can remember being charged up by playing TV video games, being outdoors, or chatting with their friends for hours on the phone. Nowadays, many of the same people are bored by those activities. Since we have more things to stimulate us nowadays, why is it a problem that some activities don't provide the same pleasure? It is because they do not give us access to pleasure twenty-four seven. Your baseline level of well-being depends on how you feel when there is nothing to stimulate you. How does it feel to be alone in a room without a smartphone? For a lot of people today, that is an uncomfortable thought.

Many of our activities add a digital layer of stimuli. When this digital layer is removed, we can quickly feel bored or uncomfortable. Try to do several things every day without any stimuli from your phone or other things that spike your dopamine, such as chewing gum or drinking coffee. Simply going for a walk without headphones can be painful if we allow ourselves to get addicted to digital stimuli. I used to live that way. I would feel unsettled doing anything without some background stimuli a few years back.

We need to feel okay without any extra stimuli to enjoy life fully. Then we can feel immense pleasure from the small pleasures in life, like a good cup of coffee. You become increasingly accustomed to the subtle pace of life when you avoid passive digital use. Your neural pathways become more sensitized, which allows you to feel more pleasure and excitement from your daily activities.

INFLUENCES

The people we surround ourselves with tremendously impact our lives: our friends, teachers, parents, family, coworkers, etc. Everything in our environment influences how we think and behave. As Jim Rohn said: "You are the average of the five people you surround yourself with the most."[20]

Since we spend a lot of time online these days, our internet activities impact us tremendously as well. You will fill your head with garbage if you spend your time reading nonsense on Reddit or watching dumbed-down videos on YouTube. Even worse, if you spend your time watching porn or doubling down on content that provokes fear and anxiety, your life will be much worse. Media outlets make money by provoking strong reactions. Why? Because images and content that generate shock value are what get the most clicks. Negative content causes stronger reactions than positive stories, which negatively affects people who consume a lot of media. You need self-control to withstand the impulse to look at certain things online that provide dopamine spikes. But equally important, you need to practice self-acceptance because it won't be perfect.

If you listen to Tony Robbins for many hours a week, your brain might perceive him as one of the most influential people in your life. That will have a positive impact on your psyche and, hopefully, your actions. Your caveman brain can't necessarily separate online influences from real life influences. Unless you seek useful information proactively online, you are constantly exposed to content that will depress and weaken you. Our thoughts are precursors to our actions. If you knew better, you would do better.

We basically only recite information we have heard or read somewhere. Very few people come to a unique understanding of the world. Almost everything we know has been taught to us by other people. So, we become like the people we surround ourselves with and the information we are exposed to. Only subject matter experts who spend their entire lives studying a narrow field find unique insights.

People like Isaac Newton, Albert Einstein, and Aristotle had original thoughts. But even they had to explore the concepts people before them had figured out. After decades of learning, they put the pieces together to produce something unique. It is unlikely that we will be much different from our influences. The point is that our environment determines our behavior and thoughts almost wholly. As a result, the content we are exposed to online affects us massively since we spend so much time there. Your consciousness will be shaped by the content you engage with online. That is also why we need to be conscious of our digital use and find content that inspires us rather than drains us. To accomplish that, we need to be disciplined and conscious.

EXERCISES

- Make a habit of pausing for thirty seconds before checking your phone when you feel an impulse or urge. Do you really have to check it, or does doing so distract you when you are bored or give you a dopamine spike you crave?
- Take a break every day for at least two hours from any digital activity. That will let you quiet your mind and get in the present moment.
- If you go into a dopamine-seeking loop, try to reflect on what kind of mental state you are in before it happens, then evaluate how you feel afterward. Awareness and

building a presence of mind is perhaps the greatest way to distance yourself from the need to check your phone.

- Reflect on your energy levels and motivation. Is there a correlation with how much time you spend online on passive activities? If you notice that a certain activity drains your energy, make a firm commitment to stop doing that. Or if you catch yourself doing it on autopilot, make sure to stop as soon as you notice it.

- Think about the content you consume online. Is it helping you grow, or is the content primarily a distraction that drains you and makes you more negative while helping you accomplish nothing? What are the most problematic ways you spend your time online? Do you have some behaviors that can turn compulsive? Make a firm commitment to access more positive content that will help you rather than drain you.

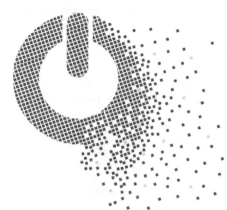

CHAPTER 2

STATISTICS ON
TECHNOLOGY OVERUSE

*Pleasures, when they go beyond a certain limit,
are but punishments.*
—Seneca

We are encouraged to stay constantly connected. Check-ing your phone one hundred times a day might be expected, but if you are more disciplined and conscious of your digital use, you will feel a tremendous positive difference. Social pressure is one of the forces working against us since almost everyone has bad habits. We tend to try to live up to other people's expectations, and going against them requires inner strength.

There is a remarkable psychological tendency called confirmation bias: we tend to ignore information that contradicts our beliefs or values while noticing and affirming information that supports our worldview. Social networks typically reward people with more of what they want. This system creates echo chambers and narrows people's field of vision. Before you know it, people cannot agree on a shared body of truths, and the political climate degrades. Strive to expose yourself to information that goes against what you believe to help combat this.

Here is a collection of research that clearly shows the adverse effects social media use and screen time in general can have on us. It is only by realizing how something affects us deep down that we are willing to let go and change.

STATISTICS ON DIGITAL USE

In 2022, the average time spent on social networking sites among internet users was 147 minutes worldwide. In 2012, the daily average was ninety minutes.[21] So we are increasingly spending more time networking online. That largely comes at the exclusion of doing it in person.

Douyin, China's version of TikTok, has set a time limit of forty minutes a day for children under fourteen.[22] This clearly shows that China takes the issues with social media seriously, and they might gain a big advantage over time by doing so.

We generally talk about ourselves 30 to 40 percent of the time when we are having conversations. On social media, that number skyrockets to 80 percent![23] Obviously, social networks change our communication patterns to be more self-absorbed. Empathy is also on the decline, which is the cornerstone of good relationships.

For people with low self-esteem, the online environment has a lot of possible triggers that can make them feel bad. Everybody else may seem happier and more popular. There are many venues for obsession, and it is really easy for the lower self to find an outlet. It is easy for the lower self to double down on feelings of inadequacy, jealousy, and so on. In addition, people who spend six hours or more on screen time daily are more likely to suffer from moderate to severe depression.[24]

A study conducted by researchers at the University of Michigan asked college students to report how they felt about their Facebook use over two weeks. The participants reported their mood and how much they had used Facebook. The study found that the more time students had spent on Facebook, the unhappier they felt. A fascinating nuance about this study is that feelings of unhappiness did not lead to using Facebook but that the more time they spent on Facebook, the unhappier they felt.[25]

An Iranian study found that excessive social media use had a significant negative influence on students' performance. A total of 360 students were enrolled in the study and the researchers concluded unequivocally that spending a lot of time on social networking can hurt your results in academia.[26] Your cognitive capacity is greatly reduced when your phone is within reach. That happens even if it is turned off.[27] It is not a reach to say that it is inadvisable to work while your phone buzzes within reach.

HOW WE SPEND OUR TIME

eMarketer estimated that in 2019, US adults used media for an average of twelve hours and nine minutes daily. These numbers involve multitasking. Examples include being on social media while watching TV or simply having the TV turned on in the background while doing something else.[28] Nonetheless, twelve hours is a staggering amount of time spent daily on digital activities.

From 1971 to 2010, a Norwegian study looked at how people aged sixteen to seventy-four spent their time on average. The study revealed that people had about one hour more leisure time every day in 2010 compared to 1971. Even so, people socialized less in 2010 than in 1971.[29] Although people generally have more leisure time now than they used to, it is mostly spent on distractions or meaningless entertainment that does not add value and actually decreases people's quality of life.

Here is something to consider. The average Netflix subscriber consumes content for seventy-one minutes every day on the platform. On average, a family spends about 35.5 minutes of quality time together (without digital devices) where they bond daily. That's half the time the average Netflix subscriber spends on Netflix![30] Of course, not all families have a Netflix subscription, but it illustrates an alarming development. We make terrible decisions about our time unless we are conscious of it. Living on autopilot is not the way to go.

Most parents believe they exemplify healthy digital habits. The truth is they are just as bad as or even worse than their kids. They know it is important for their kids' development to avoid excessive screen time, but they are not setting a good example in this area themselves. How often have you heard parents being upset about their kids playing video games? Unfortunately, the average parent spends over seven hours a day on personal screen media use (not for work).[31]

LONELINESS

Many mental health issues can be traced back to loneliness. People report that their mental health is worse than just a few years ago, with 24 percent of Americans saying their mental health is fair or poor. This is no surprise given that three out of five American adults feel lonely sometimes or always. We are living in the midst of a loneliness epidemic. The Cigna Loneliness Report revealed a correlation between loneliness and social media usage. People between ages eighteen and twenty-two—those who spend the most time on social media—are the loneliest group in America, even lonelier on average than the elderly.[32] Loneliness and weak social ties are dangerous for our health—so much so that mental health professionals have even claimed it to be equivalent to having fifteen cigarettes every day.[33] Loneliness can trigger many health issues, and people who maintain warm, loving relationships live longer.

People who limit their social media use to thirty minutes a day become happier. A study at the University of Pennsylvania investigated how limiting social media use can impact our happiness. Researchers compared a control group that used social media as usual for three weeks and another group that used social media for a maximum of thirty minutes a day. The group that limited their time on social networks felt significantly better afterward and scored lower on depression and loneliness than the control group.[34] We generally find better ways to spend our time if we stop wasting time on social media. The group that spent less time on social media also reported less fear of missing out and less anxiety. The study strongly suggests that reducing social media time to around thirty minutes a day significantly improves well-being.

Spending too much time on social networks may make us too focused on what other people think of us. When you think about it, that is how social media works. It is all about making other people think about you in a positive way. You are incentivized to get the most likes and appeal to the largest number of people. Living by intrinsic motivations rather than extrinsic ones, however, is far more enjoyable. You can be motivated by the good feeling of having a healthy, strong body or showing off your ripped physique on Instagram. It is a lot easier to sustain motivation for something you are genuinely excited about than for something you do to create impressions for others. Follow your interests, and live life in a more natural way.

Here is a nuance to be aware of: social media use may increase loneliness or reduce it, depending on how it is used. It is beneficial if it is used to organize meetings in real life. On the other hand, it can be harmful if we use it without a clear offline purpose. So, it all comes down to whether the use is proactive or passive (whether it has no real purpose offline). That is where discipline comes in again.

PROXIMITY

The phone is an easy way out of any conversation. The mere presence of a phone changes how we interact with each other.

Having phones present can turn conversations lighter, but not for the better. We instinctively sense that we may get "rejected" by people looking at their phones instead of listening to something they find boring. Deeper conversations are becoming rarer. There is less eye contact and use of body language since we spend more time communicating with screens, and the time we spend around people also gets disrupted.

Empathy and understanding are more challenging to experience with a phone present.[35] Our satisfaction from conversations is reduced, and we feel like the other person is less empathetic if they are focused on their phone during the conversation.[36] Displaying empathy requires eye contact, and anything that disrupts eye contact damages our connection with the people around us.

COMMUNICATION AND POSTURE

According to research by Mehrabian and Ferris, body language accounts for 55 percent of communication, tonality 38 percent, and words 7 percent—implying that more than 90 percent of our communication is nonverbal.[37] Using smartphones can impact our body language significantly. How often have you seen someone sitting or standing with a "text neck" with their head bent forward?

In an experiment, people were asked to interact with devices of various sizes for ten minutes. To leave after the experiment, they had to assert themselves. When people used a smartphone for ten minutes, only 50 percent were comfortable seeking out the experimenter and asserting themselves. People who interacted with the biggest device (computer) were comfortable asserting themselves a staggering 94 percent of the time. That is probably because of how interaction with various devices affects our posture.[38] It is very easy to develop a bad posture when using smartphones. Body language can influence how we feel, and since our communication is primarily based on nonverbal cues, we should be conscious of it.

SELF-STIMULATION

Because of our smartphones and constant access to the internet, we can alleviate unpleasant feelings so quickly that they almost go unnoticed. The internet is always there, for better or worse. Some people go to extremes to avoid having even a second of solitude. You can stimulate your brain infinitely and live almost like you have constant access to deep-brain stimulation. In 1986, a woman was given a chance to self-stimulate electrically, and she ended up neglecting her family, personal hygiene, and other parts of her life. She spent her time almost exclusively self-stimulating before her family intervened.[39] For some people, this tale has been repeated with the internet and video games.

HISTORICAL DEVELOPMENTS

The tendency to grossly misjudge our time is not a new thing. People wasted a lot of time before smartphones. Before the internet, we had TVs and radios. That said, never before have we spent so much time on digital content. Not only are we consuming more content than ever before, but the content is also becoming more stimulating.

In the future, the content we consume online will probably stimulate our brains even more. We will get bigger dopamine spikes, and real life will seem duller in comparison. That will fuel addiction and contribute to more wasted time. Many people are addicted to their phones already, and most have other suboptimal digital habits as well. You, as an individual, must adopt a conscious approach to digital technology. Otherwise, you will face serious consequences. We can only hope that society will help us by changing the business models of the big tech companies, but for now, we need to place the responsibility on ourselves.

People have been worried about technological advancements for a long time. The journalist Anne O'Hare McCormick described radio as having a "dazing, almost anesthetic effect upon the mind." She worried that it had made people passive in 1932![40] How far has technology advanced from those days until today? Still, people were worried about technology's impact on social relationships and our peace of mind back then.

Numerous examples of technological and medical breakthroughs had unintended consequences before regulations came. Cosmetics have previously contained harmful chemicals (and might still do in some cases), and specific medical treatments have been outright dangerous. As mentioned earlier, when we adopt a new practice or technology, there is often a delay before we understand all the good or harmful effects. Time is the best reductionist. How technology impacts our well-being certainly belongs in this discussion. It is too early to tell the full gravity of its impact on us, and many people report side effects that science cannot prove yet.

For example, when new, promising drugs come to the market, they tend to be portrayed as wonder drugs. What happens next is that people try this new drug rather carelessly. After a while, reports of people with terrible side effects come with certain treatments. Then, regulations are eventually made. Both meth and cocaine were legal for many years before being prohibited. Sigmund Freud and Pope Leo XIII, among others, used cocaine before it was outlawed.[41] Lobotomy was used as a medical treatment in the 1940s and 1950s. It was viewed as a miracle cure, even though it soon became clear that it had terrible side effects.[42]

The Nokia 3310 was released in 2000. Suddenly, people could easily text and call each other. That signaled a significant shift in our communication patterns. Still, people didn't waste much time on their phones, except for playing Snake on occasion. It was in 2007 that the first iPhone came out, propelling smartphone usage like nothing before. By 2012, most people owned a smartphone. Then, a new era began: most of us had access to all the content in the world at our fingertips.

Empathy's decline in the last two decades is likely due to loneliness from less time face-to-face and more time social networking online. Studies have shown that people who read literary fiction score higher than others on empathy since it enables us to see things from others' perspectives. Unfortunately, reading as a pastime has also declined significantly in recent years since various online activities provide more entertainment.[43]

THOUGHTS ABOUT HOW TECHNOLOGY IMPACTS US

We have to acknowledge that we live in a fantastic period. We are fortunate to have immense opportunities available, at least for many of us. Life expectancy has increased dramatically in the last century. We have become freer to be ourselves and pursue our interests as unique human beings. On top of that, we have more time away from work for leisure than people have ever had.

Survival is pretty much guaranteed in the Western world today. As recent as the 1800s, survival provided our need for purpose because it was more challenging to stay alive. We have no problem getting motivated when we must avoid real consequences like death. Lacking a solid drive can make us vulnerable to mental problems. That is why you need to find a purpose and reason for living, preferably something larger than yourself and your egoic needs. When you live in alignment with your purpose and work toward your goals, it is very difficult for negativity and depression to seep in. When we live a life of our design, it becomes less stressful, and we enjoy the challenges we encounter and are eager to overcome them.

Many athletes face issues with purpose after the end of their careers. When the crowds stop cheering, it is easy for them to resort to drugs and alcohol. The brain needs problems to overcome; otherwise, it tends to invent problems. We also become less self-centered when we have something to spend energy on. People who aren't self-centered typically have a higher sense of well-being than others.[44]

Today, there are countless ways to hide from doing difficult things. It is all too easy to hide behind screens to avoid awkward or challenging social encounters. People can avoid asking their crush out face-to-face and instead rely on digital alternatives, like messaging. Very few can tolerate high-pressure social situations since we can effectively prevent them by drinking alcohol or being passive. We are blunted when we rely on substances, making it harder to become leaders or even remotely effective. That is why we need to be more self-aware. A lot of the training that makes a person grow and become an adult is lacking because technology has made our lives easier. That doesn't mean suffering is gone. It just takes on a new psychological form if we live unconsciously.

EXERCISES

- Track your screen time during a week. Most smartphones build this feature into their settings. Also try to figure out how much time you spend on your computer. Think through how much time you could save if you only used your phone and computer for strictly necessary purposes, like answering messages and other important things. How much time could you free up? Be honest with yourself. This exercise is very important because objectivity is the foundation for change. And the numbers are probably higher than you want them to be. The point is not to beat yourself up but to get motivated enough to do something about it. It is not your fault that you have an incredibly addictive device in your pocket that you need for a lot of things. But it is your responsibility to take full ownership of how you spend your time and do what is necessary to make changes.
- Think through how you could use the extra time. What activities could you find time for? What hobbies do you want to engage in but feel like you don't have time for? Who do you wish you could spend more time with?

STATISTICS ON TECHNOLOGY OVERUSE

Which causes could you contribute time and energy to?
Think through all the things you wish you had more time
for. It is crucial to change your digital habits to find the
time for what really matters.

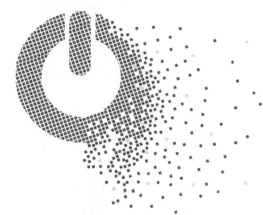

CHAPTER 3

HOW DOES THE BRAIN WORK?

Gratitude is not only the greatest of virtues,
but the parent of all the others.
—Cicero

U nderstanding how the brain works will make it much easier to change. That includes changing your digital habits, both conscious and unconscious ones.

The brain consists of nerve cells, also called neurons. Every neuron is connected to upwards of 1,000 other neurons.[45] The total number of neurons in the brain is approximately eighty-six billion.[46] Neurons are the most important parts of our nervous system. The way neurons communicate with each other is through chemical signals called neurotransmitters.

I'm going to highlight four relevant parts of the brain for the purposes of this book:

PREFRONTAL CORTEX

The prefrontal cortex (PFC) is essential for planning and decision-making. It is also involved in emotional regulation. The PFC is responsible for our willpower and requires a sufficient amount of serotonin to function optimally. It is almost impossible to have strong willpower if you have low serotonin levels. Therefore, sufficient serotonin is necessary if you want to change your life.

NUCLEUS ACCUMBENS

Activity in the prefrontal cortex regulates the activity in the nucleus accumbens and how dopamine is released there. The nucleus accumbens wants to obtain the most pleasure possible *right now*.[47] So you could say that self-control comes down to your prefrontal cortex overpowering the nucleus accumbens, which seeks immediate pleasure.

DORSAL STRIATUM

Routines and habits are controlled in the dorsal striatum, requiring dopamine to function optimally. Neurons in this brain region become denser every time we engage in a behavior. When we are stressed out, dopamine is released in this brain region, which activates our coping habits. The more stressed or anxious we get, the more the nucleus accumbens and dorsal striatum will impact our decisions.[48] That is why we typically indulge in our worst habits when we have a bad day.

THE LIMBIC SYSTEM

The limbic system is our emotional center. The limbic system consists primarily of the hippocampus, the amygdala, and the hypothalamus. To be happy, we need to satisfy the limbic system. One way to do this is through feelings of gratitude, which activate the hippocampus and amygdala. Being positive and appreciative for what we have are cheat codes for a better life. It is easy to practice appreciation as well. You just have to contemplate a few things you are happy about in your life and a few things you appreciate. Simply thinking a couple of thoughts every day that make your life better or make you feel better sounds like a pretty good deal to me.

NEURAL MOMENTUM

The different circuits in the brain work together, creating either an upward or a downward momentum. It can be hard to reverse one, good or bad. The good news is that one good incident can trigger upward momentum.[49]

Many people became isolated during COVID-19 and, as a result, lost social momentum. Something as simple as missing out on the coffee break with coworkers or working from home can be a catalyst for negative change. A minor incident can cascade into something much better or worse since it fuels momentum in our brains. The key is to put ourselves in as many situations as possible that can be a catalyst for positive momentum. Simply going for a walk every day after work can set you down a new, positive path by instilling healthy habits.

Exercise impacts our brains in many ways. It triggers neuron growth and affects the gray matter, making us mentally stronger.[50] Physical activity is one of the best things we can do to create positive momentum in our lives. The brain fuels on its momentum like a snowball rolling down a hill. If it is in motion, it will continue. Everything becomes more straightforward when the snowball starts rolling in the right direction. Sometimes you just have to take a leap of faith to make things better. Eventually, good things will start happening.

NEUROPLASTICITY

As mentioned in chapter 1, neuroplasticity is the brain's ability to change and adapt as a result of experience. Every time we do something or fail to do something, we strengthen or weaken neural pathways in our brains. A damaged function located in a part of the brain can even be moved into an area functioning normally due to the brain's ability to repair itself. The structure is changed by altering pathways.[51]

That is very good news because it means we can pretty much become what we want. If our activities reinforce what we want to become, our brain will adapt and adjust its neural pathways. The more time you spend with other people honing your social skills, the more you become a social butterfly. If you struggle with social awkwardness or shyness, you can put yourself in social situations to help you adapt and become more socially at ease. The brain can reorganize pathways and create neurons. Every time you are disciplined and do difficult things, you become stronger, and your brain adjusts, making it easier to be disciplined in the future. The scary thing with this is that the opposite is also true. Every time you take the easy way out, you become weaker and more prone to feeble behavior. That is why you should follow through on your commitments and challenge yourself. Understand that every inaction or action impacts you.

COGNITIVE BIASES

The brain has several inherent biases that shape our behavior at an unconscious level. A cognitive bias is a behavior rooted in us that is irrational. Throughout evolution, specific ways to think and behave have been beneficial for survival. For instance, it was much worse for our ancestors to spill food than to find a honeypot. Losing food could prove disastrous, which is also why we feel a stronger emotional reaction to losing than winning.

LOSS AVERSION

Loss aversion is a strong driving force behind our behaviors. On average, we feel a doubly strong emotional reaction to losing compared to winning. The fear of loss makes us act too conservatively and therefore feel like we are missing out on incredible experiences. Becoming more aware of this can make us take bigger risks, which can be a good thing in many cases. If you are young and have little responsibility, there is no reason not to try to start a business or move to a different country, for instance. But it is easy to hold ourselves back from trying these things because we are afraid of failure or looking stupid.

Loss aversion can manifest in many ways, such as holding on to a job we don't like since we are afraid of the unknown. In addition, it feels much worse to lose a penny in the stock market compared to the pleasure of acquiring one, and this tendency can fuel a lot of selling when the stock market falls and make people behave irrationally.

There is always new content that can spark our curiosity or grab our attention online. The latest video from your favorite YouTuber, news, gossip, and messages you receive fuel a never-ending cycle of fear of missing out. We even feel anxious and irritable if we cannot satisfy this compulsive need to stay connected and check our phones. In a survey, 61.4 percent of participants felt incomplete whenever they didn't bring their smartphones with them.[52]

Apps on our phones can make many daily activities obsolete or much easier. It is possible to order food on Uber Eats on your phone instead of cooking. If you feel bored, you can scroll through social media or look up things online instead of talking to people or being stimulated by your environment. You can satisfy your desires online to avoid experiencing things in real life. That basically means that every time we log on to social media when we are bored or feeling down, we are establishing a coping strategy that will increasingly disengage us from real life. We should strive to find ways to feel excited by our immediate environment.

TEMPORAL DISCOUNTING

Temporal discounting is our tendency to devalue rewards in the future for rewards right now. It is why we tend to eat candy rather than whole grain bread. We all know what the healthier option is, but sometimes we can't help ourselves, and we act based on what feels good in the moment rather than the ideal long-term.

We are wired to have a stronger preoccupation with short-term emotions rather than long-term outcomes. That has disastrous consequences for our lives over time. Most people don't have a concept of self that stretches more than six months into the future. If you manage to tip the scales in your brain and expand the time horizon you consider, your future outcomes will be a lot better. Some people are preoccupied with getting rich quickly. But they tend to stay poor since they are typically not willing to put in the necessary work to succeed. Real, lasting success typically requires years of hard work, and if you are too preoccupied with how you feel right now, there is no chance that you will be willing to work hard enough for a long enough period to get there. Success requires making it through adversity and demanding situations.

People who want financial freedom throughout their lifetime have a much higher chance of success than those who want to get rich this month. Seeking instant gratification is a bad way to live. Instead, we should strive to let go of our compulsive needs, build patience, and trust we will get there eventually.

A study looked at delay discounting between drug addicts and healthy controls. For the control group, $1,000 lost half its monetary value if they had to wait thirty-seven months before receiving the reward. Among the addicts, the reward lost half its value after only four and a half months.[53] This clearly shows that addicts care less about rewards in the future and more about what happens right now at the expense of potential future happiness, but it tends to work both ways. Many addicts manage to quit or modify their behavior if they start considering their future lives to a bigger extent. We can eliminate many of our worst impulses and make better and more rational decisions if we become connected to our future selves.

SOCIAL PROOF

Social proof is a concept that explains how we tend to follow other people's expectations, and our decision-making is strongly influenced by what others are doing. We have a basic instinct to follow other people's behavior. If you are standing, waiting for a green light and it is perfectly safe to cross the street, it can be challenging to be the first among a crowd to cross. That is because we feel an invisible pull to copy others. We fear standing out. Most people waste a lot of time online these days, making it challenging to go against the norm. Going against what most others are doing requires tolerance to social pressure.

Social proof, or the bandwagon effect, is relevant for cultivating digital discipline since you need to develop independence. Most of your friends and acquaintances probably spend a lot of passive time online. Without the ability to tolerate social pressure, you will be just like a jellyfish: when the current gets too strong in one direction, you float along regardless of your own opinion and deep-seated sense of direction. You need the ability to stand on your own two feet.

REWARD SYSTEM AND DOPAMINE

Every time you refresh Facebook on your homepage, you get exposed to new content. That takes advantage of your reward system's interest in novelty. The like button preys on our tendency to monitor our social ranking. These and other features contribute to the desensitization that occurs when we engage with social networks. If we allow something to affect our dopamine sensitivity, then we allow it to affect our desire to accomplish, get motivated, and explore.

Our brains are constantly looking for rewards in the environment. I mentioned this earlier in terms of becoming desensitized to dopamine from the constant dopamine spikes we seek through online rewards or pleasure.

A dopamine loop is a feedback loop where your dopamine system is activated and often exhausted. These loops can occur almost anywhere. Your brain can easily find endless stimulating content online and lose control, unconsciously trying to experience more stimuli. Every time we allow this to happen, we desensitize our dopamine system. Suddenly, an hour has passed and all you have done is chase the next dopamine hit. The dopamine loop is involved in many of the activities on our phones, which is why it is so easy to lose control of our attention online.

The problem is, if we don't feel complete without something, we will not feel complete with it either. That is because we will start looking for the next best thing. When we experience a craving and want something, we often want to change our internal state. If you can't avoid scrolling through social media, it is not really social media you want to indulge in; it is your inner state that you want to escape. Compulsive behavior comes from unpleasant internal states, and if we manage to transcend inner states filled with turmoil, it is much easier to avoid wasting time online. Think this through yourself. When do you usually lose control and waste hours online? Do certain situations trigger this kind of coping behavior?

You have probably heard the saying that the journey is much more important than the destination. That is because of how our brains are wired. You feel the most alive when you stay on your mission and work hard to achieve something. Then you get small drips of dopamine that fuel your motivation and excitement to keep going. The dopamine system doesn't offer satiety, which means we can never get fully satisfied by chasing and obtaining compulsive rewards, at least not for long. You will never be happy scrolling through social media or watching online videos in perpetuity, either. To get a lasting sense of well-being, stop exposing yourself to the endless triggers and dopamine loops online and build your life around activities that healthily engage your dopamine system, like reading, working out, playing the guitar, or gardening.

Following are some examples of online dopamine loops we can easily fall into:

- Watching online videos and then clicking on the recommended videos without further thought
- Constantly seeking new information with search engines by letting your mind drift
- Scrolling through social media, looking for the next exciting post
- Watching porn and looking for the next scene or picture

To have a solid work ethic, we need to release dopamine when working toward our goals. The desensitization that occurs from digital overuse ruins our ability to pick up and feel the effects of dopamine from the daily grind. Our work will not feel as satisfying, making it difficult to get things done. Try to reflect on this. Everyone's motivation fluctuates. Think about what you have done differently when you suddenly experience an upsurge or a loss of motivation. Did you feel sluggish for a few days after binge drinking? Did you spend too much time online and feel low motivation in the aftermath? Did you go hiking for a few days and felt rejuvenated afterward?

If we manage to track how different activities impact us, we can spend more time engaging in nurturing activities and less time on draining ones. Begin to evaluate how screen time specifically affects you. Did you feel better or worse after watching YouTube videos for an hour? What about reading on your Kindle?

Many people try to do a dopamine detox to reconnect with themselves. It is much easier to feel motivated to go out there in the real world and do something when we disengage from the internet. Soft skills and confidence also come from the activities we do when away from the computer. To experience a peak state, we need to put in work. Everything worth having in life requires working hard. You need to barrel through discomfort or pain before feeling a runner's high. To meet a partner, you probably have to face rejection or some awkward situations first. That is very different from how it works online. Online, you can find instant, easy pleasure or stimuli at every corner.

DECISION-MAKING

A common misconception is that we are rational. We tend to think that all our decisions are logical and that we come to conclusions after thorough contemplation—quite the opposite. We make emotional decisions and back them up with logic. A lot of our character is hidden under the surface, and we do not even fully understand what compels us. In addition, we favor short-term emotions over long-term outcomes because of temporal discounting. Many people prefer instant money when given a choice between fifty dollars immediately or one hundred dollars one year from now. Where can you find a 100 percent guaranteed return annually?

The activities that generally give us the most pleasure have a startup cost. Things like hiking, swimming, and going to a restaurant with friends are enjoyable activities for most people. When we get around to them, they satisfy us much more than simply swiping our cell phones. *Easy* is our biggest enemy. We end up losing so much time on activities that give us temporary, illusionary fun compared to activities that give us true satisfaction. Smartphones have made it much easier to go for the easy option. It is important to remind ourselves that the small startup cost of many activities is preferable to easy, digital alternatives.

Let's say you value what happens right now compared to what happens in five years at a ratio of 5:1. That means that you value what happens right now five times more than what happens in five years. To offer an example, let's assume this is the default of how people discount rewards. If you somehow managed to switch this balance to 2:1, you would start to behave very differently. Now you would suddenly think much more about how your actions right now affect your future. To some people, this sounds boring. If you are among them, you are wasting your future potential. If you shift your perspective to care more about the future than you do now, you probably won't have as much fun in the next few weeks or the next few months, but the rest of your life will be much better.

You will experience more pleasure and happiness overall by caring more about the future. The only downside is that we have to decline some treats at the moment. Where do you want to be in five years? What about ten years? What do you need to do right now to get there? Shifting our perspective this way can be a powerful aid to change our digital habits at a fundamental level.

NEGATIVE SELF-ESTEEM

People compare themselves to others endlessly. We are incredibly social animals that form intricate social networks. That has contributed to Meta becoming one of the biggest companies in the world. We are constantly trying to figure out our social worth compared to others. Knowing your social value has always been crucial for survival. It is still essential for mate selection, friendships, and happiness, among other things, but it is not as vital for survival as it once was. Still, we spend enormous amounts of time making ourselves miserable following the urge to determine our social worth online.

Our tendency to be too self-conscious also gets us into trouble. We think people will laugh and talk about us endlessly if we post something that doesn't get that much praise and likes. Most people tend to focus on themselves. If you post a photo that doesn't receive as many likes as you want, you will probably overvalue how this impacts other people. Other people will not care; they will focus on themselves. We are driven to perfect images and give ourselves a perfect impression in social media feeds. As a result, people's lives look much better on social media than they probably are.

You can start behaving more rationally if you become aware of our inherent psychological tendencies. In addition, you will not be as vulnerable to the manipulation the media and digital platforms are capable of. You will see the world and yourself more objectively and start thinking more for yourself. Going a bit deeper is required to change your behavior at the surface level.

EXERCISES

- Can you think of any situations or choices you have made in your life where you have been too short-sighted (temporal discounting)? Awareness is the key to overcoming these tendencies, as well as having a longer time frame. What about situations where you have been too conservative and didn't take the chances you should (loss aversion)?
- Think how your life would be different today if you had behaved more rationally in the past. Would your finances be better? What about your relationships?

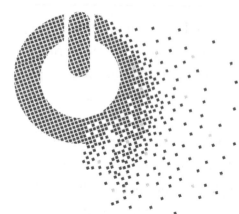

CHAPTER 4

HOW TECHNOLOGY EXPLOITS US

Addiction is a progressive narrowing of the things that bring you pleasure . . . a good life is a progressive expansion of the things that bring you pleasure.
—Andrew Huberman

U sing the internet changes our brains because of neuroplasticity. When we surf online, our brains are activated in certain ways that initiate changes. If we can control how we focus our attention, we can more easily control how we feel. Having a centered mind is necessary for happiness and feeling at peace.

Whenever we let our minds drift off online, we train our minds to become less centered. The internet is basically a huge party for our brains because of the endless pleasure available.

VARIABLE REWARDS

All the big platforms we spend a lot of time on, such as TikTok, Snapchat, and Facebook, take advantage of our neural wiring. B. F. Skinner found that the strongest way to reinforce certain behaviors is to provide random rewards. When we are trying to get an outcome but don't know when it will come is when we are the most motivated. Variable rewards release the most dopamine. Rewards predictably scheduled seem boring because we know what to expect. Our dopamine levels don't fluctuate as much. But when the reward is unpredictable, we can easily lose control of ourselves.[54]

We constantly check our phones because we never know if we will be rewarded or not. Maybe a hot guy or girl has sent a message on Tinder, or you have received a Snap from your crush. Perhaps your brother has texted you. All these possibilities make our dopamine fluctuate wildly. The notifications give us dopamine spikes. Swiping online dating apps, checking your email, and checking social networks for updates are similar to playing a slot machine. Companies like Meta have spent billions of dollars perfecting their digital slot machines.

TECH COMPANIES: THE MASTER MANIPULATORS

Interruptions are good for business for the big tech companies—omnipresence and taking as much of our time as possible is ideal. Snapchat wants you to experience a sense of urgency in responding to messages. That is why they have daily streaks and other features to make us respond rapidly— and if we don't, we fear social consequences, such as seeming uninterested. Platforms like Snapchat aren't designed to help you live a balanced life.

Snapchat is gamifying friendships and communication to make us spend time on their platform. People are afraid to abandon Snapstreaks (a feature that requires you and another person to continue communicating within twenty-four hours or else you lose the streak). The result is that Snapchat generates enormous amounts of traffic based on fear and anxiety. Suppose Snapchat was to introduce a reward for those who sent more than twenty Snaps to each other every day. In that case, we could see teenagers using this new feature as an important measurement of the strength of their relationships. That is how intertwined the platform has become in communication with certain demographics.

Some of the social indicators used to determine the strength of relationships have been moved from real life to social media. Did someone like your picture from way back? That could be a sign that they really like you. It is becoming more normal to communicate indirectly as we have a lot of digital alternatives that allow us to avoid potentially awkward encounters or subjects in real life.

Wealthy people generally value their time above everything else. That is because we are free to spend our time in whatever way we want when we reach a certain level of success. However, our life is only a series of moments regardless of our income or net worth. In the attention economy, our time and attention are the products. We are not actually getting more time. Reed

Hastings, CEO of Netflix, summed this up perfectly when he said their main competitor is actually sleep.[55] If digital platforms manage to increase the time we spend online in order to increase their revenue, we will have less time and energy to spend on the things that matter.

INCENTIVES

Incentives motivate us or encourage us to do something. When structuring a company, it is essential to incentivize people to behave in a way that aligns with the company's interests. People typically follow the incentives as they want to get rewarded for what they do. A typical employee doesn't necessarily see the big picture but tends to act aligned with their reward structure.

Successful business owners, entrepreneurs, and leaders understand this very well. People tend to work harder when there are bonuses to motivate them. An excellent example of the importance of incentives is FedEx, the transportation giant. They used to pay drivers who transported goods by the hour. Then they streamlined their operation by paying workers for *the entire shift* instead. That proved to work very well.[56] If you want to go bankrupt, give employees incentives misaligned with the company's interests, and you will be out of business quickly.

Certain behaviors are incentivized on social media, such as self-promotion. It is all about showing off and portraying oneself in the best possible way. That can lead to narcissism. In a way, narcissism is a lack of awareness of the world and people around us. It is natural that this can result from spending too much time online as we spend less time observing the world around us and more time on social networks, where everything revolves around how we look to others. Narcissism is not a stable personality trait; rather, our environments influence our level of narcissism, and we find ourselves in different places on the spectrum.

Social media also portrays success as effortless. Successful people show off their leisure time in the Bahamas. The years of grinding and sacrifice required to become successful, however, are not portrayed as openly. That can give us unrealistic expectations, and many people fail to understand the sacrifices behind the shiny Instagram posts. Social media is all about making things seem easy and perfect, and many people hide their vulnerabilities. But the things that aren't perfect are what bind us together. When we dare to show our weaknesses and avoid trying to be perfect, we become relatable and capable of connecting with others deeply.

The human brain tends to focus more strongly on negative events than positive ones because it is more critical for survival to avoid heated conflicts, a tiger, or war than to have pleasurable experiences. Marketers rely on causing cognitive dissonance and emotional reactions to make us feel unhappy and discontent so that we will buy their products. We feel a much stronger urge to buy something if we are in a negative emotional state compared to a neutral one. That makes it easier to present a solution to the problem.

DOPAMINE'S ESSENTIAL ROLE IN MOTIVATION

Neuromarketing is the study of how to capitalize on the brain's neural wiring. As you know, dopamine is released when we reach rewards, such as sex and food, and are working to secure them. Effective marketing takes advantage of this by exploiting deeply rooted sexual and social reward structures in our brains.

Drug abuse downregulates dopamine receptors and dopamine production. Abusers always chase the first high, and achieving the same sensation later becomes more difficult because the pleasure system becomes overstimulated. Addicts have less capacity to experience pleasure from other things. In fact, the side effects of addiction are partly a result of decreased reward sensitivity. Dopamine fluctuations are critical aspects of our reward system and our motivation. Dopamine is so vital for motivation that overstimulated lab mice lose the motivation to feed themselves. They will still feel pleasure if they are fed, but they won't go out to feed themselves.

Having an overstimulated dopamine system can be disastrous for our well-being. Unfortunately, when we are using our phones or computers, we spend most of our time on platforms that are made to exploit our dopamine system. The problem with this is that we end up desensitized, and many people experience mild symptoms of addiction in their daily lives that they don't trace back to internet use. For example, before I cultivated digital discipline, I used to check my phone first thing in the morning and spend a few minutes online before doing anything else. Throughout the day, I would check my phone as soon as I got bored or whenever I felt anxious. Before going to bed, I would stay on the phone for hours watching porn, movies, or something else that gave me very little—except instant pleasure. In the beginning, when I tried to avoid looking at the phone constantly, I would experience withdrawal symptoms, such as anxiety, cravings, and a depressed mood. It was almost impossible to stay away.

On the flip side, we experience increased levels of circulating dopamine when we meditate.[57] Meditation is essentially about quieting the mind and becoming centered. The purpose is to reach a point where you can be satisfied without any stimuli. It isn't easy to slow down in a fast-paced world, but life becomes better when we manage to wind down and find pleasure in simple activities. When we find the time for activities like reading, going for a walk, writing, playing board games, or gardening, we give our brains the chance to adjust to subtler pleasures. In addition, we quiet our minds, and the stillness we sorely lack today is the key to happiness. Not thinking is the ideal state without racing thoughts about the past or future. Only by leaving the never-ending digital buzz behind can we get into that state.

By forcing dopamine production inside the reward system of rats, it is possible to reduce the self-administration of drugs.[58] If we somehow manage to increase our dopamine levels, we will be better equipped to avoid mindless digital consumption. It is much easier to end up scrolling mindlessly for hours if we are tired and unmotivated. You know that you have healthy dopamine levels if you feel excited by the tasks and things you do in daily life. I am aware that my motivation and excitement in my everyday life highly depend on how much time I spend scrolling mindlessly online. If I am disciplined, my brain starts adjusting, and it is much easier to get excitement from other places.

People with Parkinson's disease produce too little dopamine and can have trouble performing simple tasks. If they separate tasks into subtasks, it gets easier to accomplish what they want. If a person with Parkinson's is lying in bed and wants to make breakfast, this can be too difficult. Too many steps are involved in releasing the necessary dopamine to finish all the subtasks needed to make breakfast. On the other hand, success will be much more likely if the first goal is to get out of bed, the second is to get out of the room, the third is to go down the stairs, etc. That shows the importance of dopamine in everything we do.

The activities abused the most by humans increase dopamine. Drug use, watching porn, gambling, and anything that can provide strong dopamine hits can make us addicted. We have the option to administer dopamine hits to ourselves constantly at will with digital devices. Interestingly, people often report that they become more productive by reducing mindless digital consumption. It is no wonder when we understand how dopamine functions.

Neuroscientist Andrew Huberman has described addiction in an amazing way: "Addiction is a progressive narrowing of the things that bring you pleasure," and "a good life is a progressive expansion of the things that bring you pleasure."[59] A progressive expansion can happen if we self-regulate and gradually find joy once again in simpler things by avoiding intense stimuli. In the world we live in, this is all about managing to regulate ourselves from overconsuming stimuli from porn, drugs, alcohol, junk food, and screens. If we self-regulate, dopamine will drive us forward and motivate us to achieve and experience incredible things. Or, as I like to put it, our capacity to feel pleasure is inversely proportional to how overstimulated we are.

Technology is moving ahead rapidly, and it will continue to do so. Screens are produced in higher resolution almost yearly. Neuromarketers get even better at predicting our behavior and luring us in. Our digital habits become more ingrained as time goes by. As a result, every time the technological interfaces we engage with become more stimulating, our lives away from them will seem duller by comparison.

Elon Musk said: "If you assume any rate of improvement at all, then games will become indistinguishable from reality."[60] The time to cultivate digital discipline is now.

Most people do not properly understand the negative impact certain online behaviors can have on us. Not only do they waste our time, but they also do profound harm that is difficult to detect. Procrastination kills our self-esteem, and it is incredibly easy to waste time on YouTube or checking Snapchat every five minutes to postpone reading for an exam. It might not seem like a big deal right then and there to choose to watch a short video clip, but these choices chip away at our self-esteem. Our smartphones have made it much easier to turn into a weak, feeble man-child—just as I had become with my addiction.

Adolescents and children grow up with screen time integral to their upbringing. Screens are with them at school and even during their time with their parents and friends. Because our prefrontal cortices are not fully developed until approximately age twenty-five, children are very vulnerable to becoming addicted to video games and other digital activities.[61] What happens with children's emotional, social, and cognitive development when so much time is spent interacting with screens rather than people? What happens with adults' development?

EMOTIONAL TRIGGERS

Smartphones provide a way for many people to manage uncomfortable emotional triggers. They allow us to avoid looking inside ourselves when we are feeling stressed, sad, or lonely. Our phones can soothe pretty much any emotion. If you feel lonely, you can start chatting with some friends. If you feel stressed, you can watch videos on YouTube. Getting a quick fix rather than addressing the root of the problem fixes nothing, though. Running away from a problem is not the road to a happy life. We need to take a deep and honest look at ourselves from time to time. That is becoming more difficult in a connected world since everything is getting shallower and more superficial.

People would rather experience uncomfortable electric shocks than be alone without anything to do. How crazy is that? In an experiment, people were asked to sit and be alone with their thoughts for fifteen minutes. They had the chance to give themselves an electric shock to escape the boredom and got the opportunity to try the device that provided the shocks beforehand. Among those who reported that they would be willing to pay money not to feel the pain of the shock, 25 percent of women and two-thirds of men gave themselves a shock voluntarily during the fifteen minutes.[62]

How could people possibly prefer electric shocks over relaxation? Most likely, it is because they find solitude more painful than the slight pain of shocks. Many people rely so much on stimuli in their everyday lives that short periods of solitude without the phone or computer are painful. When we avoid time by ourselves without electronic stimuli of some kind at all costs, it is no wonder that we find it uncomfortable. In moments of privacy, we also find the time to go deeper within ourselves to resolve internal issues. The way to resolve internal problems is to acknowledge how we feel and then find ways to accept them and transcend them. Running away from internal problems only ensures that they remain unresolved. When we pick up our smartphones during the day, we often do so to avoid facing our inner thoughts and demons.

We have tremendous economic abundance in the Western world, as well as great opportunities, but we can forget to fulfill the social intimacy we crave so deeply. The competing influence of screens leaves us with less quality time for the people closest to us. We should strive to live a lifestyle that satisfies our primitive needs. We are adapted to a very different environment than we live in today. To thrive, we need to understand and then realign ourselves to how our tribal ancestors lived. We need to listen to our bodies' signals. It is much easier to be attuned to these signals if you have a healthy relationship with digital devices.

ACTIVE AND PASSIVE CONSUMPTION

We mentioned earlier that there are two kinds of screen time: active and passive. They affect our brains in very different ways. Passive screen time is associated with anxiety and mood disorders, while active use is not. Coding, creating websites, creating music, writing, reading useful articles, watching educational content, and so on are all very good. Consuming videos passively is not. Educational screen time has no negative relation to other parts of life. Passive screen time, however, has a plethora of adverse effects, such as declining mental and physical health.[63]

THE GREAT SMARTPHONE EXPERIMENT

In the attention economy, everything is centered around the number of views one gets. It is all about being more captivating than the person next to you. We clearly see some adverse effects a decade into the great smartphone experiment. We spend a worrying amount of time hunched over, scrolling through feeds that we will never recall. A lot of our time is spent on things that have no real meaning for us at the end of the day.

What will the result of this transformation be? Will everyone be sitting in their rooms having virtual sex with a porn star? Is technology like agriculture when it was invented? It made the rulers rich, but many were forced to work as slaves to make the elite wealthy. Is the same thing happening with social media in a disturbing way?

DELAYED OR INSTANT GRATIFICATION?

We all crave the experience of neurochemical highs from dopamine and serotonin. We can experience these pleasant spikes in our everyday lives by having fabulous experiences and building a future for ourselves, or we can complain and be passive entertainment consumers.

With technology, we basically have shortcuts for everything; this is not good in many cases. You can watch a movie instead of traveling or having a new, exciting real life experience. You can go out and try to meet someone or stay in front of the computer and please yourself. You can take drugs, drink alcohol, watch TV, or numb yourself in any way you want. You can do many things to avoid facing difficult choices or do something with your life. You can complain and find things that aren't perfect yet.

You experience a high when you complain, similar to what you experience if you resolve the issue. It is not as big, but this is why complaining makes taking action almost impossible. When we remain quiet, we can solve the task at hand. If we complain first, we have already experienced the neurochemical high we crave, and action feels unnecessary. Many people are overwhelmed with opportunities yet prefer staying home and finding the negatives instead.

With many of our choices, we can go for immediate or delayed gratification. The more we manage to postpone rewards, the better off we will be in the future. Saying no to that ice cream can feel painful, but it becomes a lot easier when there is a goal of getting into better shape.

We all strive for neurochemical rewards. But there are different ways to go about reaching them. You can form bonds and friendships with interesting people, fulfilling your desire to feel close and connected to others. This feeling is created by oxytocin. It is also possible to find others and complain together to experience oxytocin. Doing this will give you a neurochemical reward in the short-term. Isn't it much better to decline this hit for a period and build the life you have always dreamed of instead? If you train yourself to decline some of these hits in the short-term, you will be in a great position to thrive later. If you decline the option to take the easy way out, you will naturally work toward real goals instead.

Digital media and many other things in society provide neu-rochemical rewards that require little or no effort these days. But the things in life that matter are hard to obtain. Finding your dream partner is no walk in the park. A lot of work is required to maintain a great relationship over many years. Sacrifice and long hours are necessary to excel in your craft or career. It becomes easier every year to experience neurochemical rewards with digital media, but building a skill set or working hard remains the same. That is why we need to be conscious of our digital use.

EXERCISE

- Think through a few situations where you tend to go for either instant or delayed gratification. Reflect on how it feels afterward. Often, it is only a good feeling temporarily to go for instant rewards, and you would feel better in the long run if you chose delayed gratification.

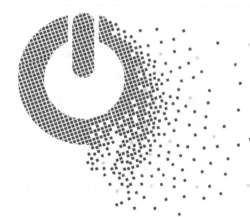

CHAPTER 5

WHAT MAKES US HAPPY?

*The happiness of those who want to be popular depends
on others; the happiness of those who seek pleasure
fluctuates with moods outside their control; but the
happiness of the wise grows out of their own free acts.*
—Marcus Aurelius

Many things have a significant impact on our happiness.
Among them are our relationships, financial stability, lifestyle, career, and health. In this chapter, we will dive deeply into
the neurochemical basis for happiness and how we can become
happier by optimizing our neurotransmitters. It is challenging to
define happiness since it encompasses so many things. The defi-

nition we use in this book has two components. One is a deeper sense of satisfaction, and the other is feeling good emotions and pleasure. Both are very important for our subjective well-being.

Spending too much time online can be detrimental to both components of happiness, and we will look more into why and then uncover strategies to become happier and more content. Luckily, we can quickly change our level of happiness and satisfaction in life by making better, more conscious decisions.

STATISTICS ON HAPPINESS

General happiness among US adults is on the decline, and it has been declining since the 1970s. Among US adolescents, happiness was on the rise until about 2012, when it started dropping significantly. Can you think of something else that happened between 2011 and 2012? Well, smartphones became widespread, and most people bought one during this period. Nowadays, young people spend less time socializing, sleeping, and reading than they used to. It is no wonder that happiness has been declining. Sleep and social time are bedrocks for our well-being, and screen time has been affecting this.[64] We don't magically get more time than people before us, either—we are sacrificing our time and health for meaningless online activity.

In a large study, Jean M. Twenge and W. Keith Campbell examined digital habits and well-being among forty thousand children and adolescents. They used various well-being measures and looked at different kinds of screen time. The researchers found that many side effects began appearing after more than one hour a day of screen time. Among them were less self-control, impaired focus, lower emotional stability, and worse outcomes with friendships. Non-users and those with low screen time did not differ much in well-being.[65] That clearly supports the notion that conscious, limited use is the way to go. When we are disciplined with our digital use, few side effects tend to appear.

HAPPINESS AND SOCIAL RELATIONSHIPS

Relationships are the biggest source of happiness and positive emotions for many people. Those with rich social relationships tend to be happy with their lives. We are less social nowadays than in decades before since more people live alone, and screen time replaces or jeopardizes some of our social time. We all need time with other people. When introverts are more outgoing, they typically enjoy it and get surprised by how good they feel about the social interaction afterward.

Our ancestors lived in tribes with close social ties. These ties are fading away in the modern social environment. We are meant to be active and closely connected to other people. However, we can regain control of our lives and live life to its fullest if we want to. Being active with other people combines two of the most important things we can do for our well-being. Activities like playing soccer or just going for a run with a group of people are great for us.

CIRCUMSTANCES AND PURPOSE

Even though genetics play a role in determining happiness, we can turn specific genes off or on as we grow and change. We have the ultimate power to change our lives the way we want to. Even if only 10 percent of our happiness were within our control, it would be meaningless not to optimize our lives. Ten percent is a huge difference. In reality, it is more like 90 percent of our happiness is in our control. We can change how we look at things, learn new things, and build better habits. Our actions, attitudes, and thoughts are among the most important factors for happiness.

Having a sense of purpose is not to be underestimated when it comes to happiness either.[66] If what you do today aligns with where you want to end up long-term, you have vertical coherence. Happy and mentally healthy people tend to have a high degree of vertical coherence. Much of our cognitive dissonance comes from doing things we know are not in our long-term best interests.

DISTRACTION VS. DEEP SATISFACTION

With constant access to distractions, it is easy to satisfy the surface-level need for pleasure and overlook our deeper need for internal satisfaction. Deeper satisfaction comes with reflection, integrity, resilience, strong social bonds, and overall living a life that satisfies you. If you numb yourself by looking at social media for hours every day, it is easy to lose track of clarity and purpose. You need to allow time for reflection to stay connected to your vision in life. And how can we expect to control our happiness if we can't effectively manage our attention? Happiness is a lot about focusing on the positives. That is why losing control of our attention can be such a big problem. When we surf the web or scroll on our phones, we tend to lose control of our attention. That makes us less capable of positively directing our thoughts, which is also about mindfulness and not letting the mind drift off.

Social media is more self-focused than others-focused, which is required when communicating in real life. Focusing on the well-being of others is highly important for our happiness. Going beyond ourselves and focusing on others is the key to many things in life. Shifting your awareness this way will enable you to obtain more influence and make you more relaxed and carefree. Focusing too much on ourselves is not healthy, and many of us would benefit from avoiding it.

Social media offers the drifting mind endless chances to fall prey to temptations and distractions. Every time you get distracted, you are making it easier to become distracted in the future as well. Being able to focus is tremendously important. Whether you want to thrive in your career or education or become good at a sport, you need to be able to focus deeply.

FOCUS AND HAPPINESS

We can change our emotions in an instant with thoughts and our physiology. We can recall pleasant memories or ask ourselves empowering questions: "What am I excited about in my life right now? What are some things I love? How does this make me feel?" Happiness is closely linked to our posture and how we use our bodies. By changing our posture, we can develop more resourceful states of mind. The common denominator here is that we need a centered mind and the ability to control our attention to have the option to change our emotional state. Becoming happier is something we can do at will by changing how we focus.

NEUROTRANSMITTERS AND HAPPINESS

Four neurotransmitters are crucial to our happiness: serotonin, dopamine, oxytocin, and endorphins. Gut microbiota is involved in producing neurotransmitters, so having a healthy gut is also very important.[67] You can take probiotics to stimulate your gut health, and this can actually help increase your well-being.[68] If you have poor gut health, it will influence how the bacteria metabolize the amino acids in food into neurotransmitters.

SEROTONIN

Serotonin relates to social dominance and our inner sense of security. It is released when we feel respected by others, gain social importance, or feel like we belong to a group. Increasing serotonin levels is closely linked to accomplishing activities that reinforce self-esteem as well. That is pretty much the opposite of browsing the internet passively. It is easy to start comparing ourselves to other people on social media, which can make us feel worse about ourselves. Practicing gratitude, on the other hand, increases serotonin and is one of the easiest ways to become happier. You will become happier by taking a minute each day to think about a few things you are grateful for. "Gratitude is not only the greatest of virtues, but the parent of all the others," stated Cicero.

DOPAMINE

By now, you should be familiar with dopamine. Dopamine relates to pleasure seeking and the feelings associated with accomplishment. It is released when we engage in reward-seeking behavior and motivates us to work toward our goals. Gratitude also increases dopamine.[69] If we overstimulate the dopamine system, we can feel apathetic and lose drive and determination. That will also damage our happiness significantly. We need to self-regulate our consumption online to ensure healthy dopamine levels in order to thrive.

OXYTOCIN

Oxytocin (the bonding chemical) is released when we bond and connect with other people. Touch is very effective at increasing oxytocin. That does not happen when we text others; it happens when we talk to them or spend time face-to-face.[70] Researchers at the University of Wisconsin-Madison showed that stressed-out children who interact with their mothers via instant messages don't release oxytocin. In fact, their cortisol levels (stress levels) were as high as those who didn't interact with their parents.[71] On the other hand, children who spoke with their mothers on the phone released oxytocin and calmed down. We lose a lot when we replace in-person social encounters with messages. We lose out on genuine connection and feel more isolated. Oxytocin reduces our need for stimuli. Replacing the visit to the coffee shop with your friends with a conversation on WhatsApp or Messenger is not a good idea. Social support is crucial to both avoiding and treating addiction. Without strong social ties, it is much easier to experience addiction and fall prey to compulsive behavior.

ENDORPHINS

Endorphins are released to mask pain, which is why they are known as the body's natural pain reliever. They are responsible for a "runner's high." When we laugh, endorphins are released as well. Overusing the internet makes us more prone to becoming sedentary, which could negatively affect our endorphin levels.

Excessive exposure to digital environments can lead to lower levels of all the primary neurotransmitters that control the happiness factor. We can desensitize our dopamine system with passive digital use. Deficient vitamin D levels and melatonin levels caused by too much screen time indoors harm serotonin production.[72] Also, less time spent around other people can come at the cost of decreased oxytocin and serotonin levels. Physical activity and being outdoors are also traded for more screen time. These choices have a detrimental impact on our health.

THE LIMBIC SYSTEM

As mentioned in chapter 3, if you want to be happy, you need to satisfy the limbic system—the emotional center of our brain that's responsible for our feelings.[73] If we remain active and social and unplug from the digital world as much as possible, we are much more likely to satisfy the limbic system and feel good. Sitting on the couch watching TV alone is pretty much the opposite of what we should do to satisfy our limbic system, but that is what most people do every evening. It requires a certain degree of awareness and willpower to make sure your lifestyle is compatible with how the limbic system rewards you.

PRODUCTIVE WAYS TO SPEND YOUR TIME

We have an ideal trade-off between different activities for our happiness. It is the trade-off between time spent working out, engaging with friends and family, working, traveling (and more) that maximizes our unique preferences. This balance is different for everyone.

Let's say we have a friend named John who is forty-two years old and has a wife and a son. He earns a good salary, so the family is financially secure, and he doesn't have to work long, excessive hours. He spends eight hours a day at work, and he finds the work challenging and rewarding. John also values moments with his son and wife and would like to spend a lot of quality time with them. When he has alone time, he enjoys going for runs and riding his bike. John spends time with his friends weekly, playing poker or just hanging out. He also enjoys reading, but he feels like he doesn't have time for it anymore.

For John, spending the right amount of time doing what he values is ideal. For most people, this involves quite a bit of time being social since we are social creatures. It also involves various projects and hobbies for many people. What happens when we spend three to four hours daily on our cell phones? Is suddenly time spent on our cell phones one of the most important pillars for our subjective happiness? Most likely not. It just steals time from the other things we could have been doing that would have yielded a significantly higher return. It will most likely make us lose out on time with our family or, at the very least, reduce the quality of the time we spend around them. People derive less pleasure from their relationships when cell phones are present, and parents experience less social connection with their children.[74]

Excessive use of smartphones leaves us with less time to do the things we value. Maybe even worse is that we are penalized neurochemically by the usage. We have to consider alternative costs to how we spend our time. Many people these days have behavioral addictions and use screen time on damaging activities, such as losing money on gambling or fueling shopping addictions.

TALKING WITH STRANGERS AND THE CONNECTION TO HAPPINESS

Previously, I mentioned that our smartphone addictions often prevent us from talking to strangers while waiting in lines. It may surprise you to know that conversations with strangers significantly impact our well-being. There are two important reasons for this. First, we are incredibly social and release a lot of feel-good neurotransmitters when we spend time with people. In addition, we reinforce a healthy and empowering worldview when we talk to strangers. If you engage in small talk with strangers, you do so because you have optimistic assumptions about the world. If you never engage with strangers, it is much easier to think that they are out to get you since you miss out on the typically pleasant experience of talking with them. In an experiment, researchers asked commuters on trains and buses to connect with the person beside them or remain disconnected. The researchers found that people had the best experience on their commutes when they connected with others, contrary to what they thought.[75] Don't default to checking your smartphone when you are waiting in line. Look for people open to small talk.

WELL-BEING

Our lives are not siloed; everything ties in together. It is tough to do anything well if we don't feel at ease within ourselves. Excelling academically or in our careers largely depends on our ability to focus. Our focus is again reliant on how we feel within ourselves. Sitting down and reading a book will be easy if you feel at ease. When a feeling of inner peace and comfort is present, we can easily focus, and we don't have to use as much force to get the job done.

Ideally, we should reach a place where doing activities that nurture us financially, spiritually, and socially feels good. Most people find going for a run a challenge. Others feel the same way about work or reading. It is possible to engage in activities like these that are helpful for us long-term and get pleasure from them. That requires crossing a few barriers to entry, though.

People can experience the same situations differently. For some, walking to work in the morning is a pleasant experience. Feeling the wind in their hair and looking at people and their surroundings can be satisfying. For others, it is painful to be outside in the cold, walking to work. They need more potent stimuli to feel okay since their brain circuits are more desensitized. Luckily, it is possible to sensitize your brain! It is supposed to be pleasurable to *be* in your body. By being consistently conscious of the stimuli you allow in your life, you will find more pleasure in the small things you experience with time. It will be hard in the beginning, like it was when I gave up unnecessary digital stimuli, but if you just keep going, things will get easier.

Because everyone experiences life in a unique way, there are huge differences in people's subjective well-being. This is easy to decipher based on what people are talking about, what they are focusing on, and how they look and behave. If you spend too much time on distractions, you can increase your subjective well-being by becoming conscious of your digital use. If you force yourself to be without your cell phone or other sources of digital stimuli over and over, your inner state will begin to shift. You will eventually learn to become your source of good emotions rather than relying on entertainment from others.

As I've mentioned, we have a lot of tools at our disposal to suppress discomfort, pain, boredom, or any negative feeling. You can check your smartphone to escape boredom or loneliness. You can have a few beers to numb yourself. You can lie down on the couch and watch TV to avoid discomfort. You can drive instead of walking in the rain. By constantly avoiding the inevitable pain that is a part of existence, we do ourselves a grave disservice. Running away from pain only makes it appear in a different form later.

We are at our best when we are centered, present, and in alignment with ourselves. To become centered, we need to have moments of deep presence daily. That can be obtained most easily when we also take time-outs from the digital world. It is much easier to reconnect with ourselves when we take some time to become present and leave the never-ending online buzz alone.

THE SOCIAL BEING

Our relationships impact our physical and mental health tremendously. We need time to connect with friends and family. When we spend time with our friends and loved ones, we constantly share little details about our lives, and this intimacy is sorely needed. It makes us feel like there is a point to existing. Our neocortex is larger than that of any other primate, and when we are social, it is constantly firing. Society, as we know it today, is essentially a result of cooperation—a social behavior. Collaboration has taken us to the top of the food chain. Physical contact, socializing, and simply being around people have a myriad of benefits. We are the happiest when we are around other people and feel connected to them.

Feeling connected and belonging to a group is important for our well-being. Being around other people instills a sense of responsibility and concern for others. Bonds and connections with others can also help us feel a greater sense of purpose and reduce stress. When we feel safe about our social relationships, we feel good because of serotonin. Social isolation and perceived low status increase stress (cortisol). The most isolated people are at the most risk of experiencing many health issues, and our resilience largely depends on social bonds.

Social norms have changed extremely fast in the last ten to twenty years. It is far easier to slide a direct message to someone than go up and talk to them in real life. We are getting worse at reading subtle social nuances since we spend less time being social than before. In the future, we might know just the right emoji for a situation but not necessarily the proper facial expression.

Communication is at the core of business success, education, and social relationships of any kind, and our social skills are undoubtedly the most important skill we learn. John D. Rockefeller (the wealthiest man in American history) said: "The ability to deal with people is as purchasable a commodity as sugar or coffee, and I will pay more for that ability than for any other under the sun."[76]

We will need to communicate well and deal with other people regardless of where technology takes us. We are still the social animal, and we should not let screens steal the time we should have spent being social. If we do, we pay for it with our happiness.

EXERCISE

- Find your ideal trade-off between time spent on different activities. Write down your favorite things to do and how often you get to do them (this will fluctuate with time). Do you wish you had more time? If so, reflect on whether your digital habits limit your time for family, friends, exercise, or something else. Commit to spending more time on these things.

PART 2

CHAPTER 6

THE KEYS TO HABIT CHANGE

Mere gossip anticipates real talk, and to express what is still in thought weakens action by forestalling it.
—Søren Kierkegaard

Identifying underlying thoughts and insights can help you change your digital habits. By understanding and emotionally accepting the harsh truths of life, you are much more likely to modify your behavior.

GROWING UP TODAY

Many people watch Netflix or play video games daily for hours, living in a fairy-tale delusion. Youngsters grow up and are prepared for adulthood later than in previous generations. Growing up involves sacrifices and taking on responsibility, but it is easy to avoid taking on responsibility these days.

As a young man or woman today, it can be difficult to sacrifice freedom for responsibility. A child has all the potential in the world; they can be anything. As we grow older, we lose some potential and are forced to make a sacrifice, whether we want to or not. When there are seemingly endless opportunities, it can be difficult to pick something. Young people today experience an extended period of adolescence. By delaying taking on responsibility, we actually sacrifice something much bigger than if we had chosen something earlier.

The ability to choose is closely linked to self-esteem. If we cannot trust our decisions, we will constantly second-guess them, making it difficult to make big decisions. Because it is easier than ever to meet our basic needs in the Western world, making decisions usually isn't life or death. Unlike our ancestors, we encounter fewer threatening situations and have to make fewer high-stakes decisions. Earlier generations had to start working sooner and take on a lot of household responsibility much earlier as well. Therefore, it isn't easy to develop enough self-esteem to take on the big responsibilities of adult life at the same age as our parents and grandparents did.

When we are young, we have the chance to be everything, and it can be challenging to let this vision of ourselves go. You can be a firefighter, you can be a cop, you can travel the world, or you can work at a coffee shop five minutes from your home. When we abandon choosing, we are selecting an inferior option. Giving up all the possibilities in the world and choosing something means that some of our wishes and aspirations die. We can't fulfill them all. That is why video games, porn, and other easy pleasures are so compelling. They allow pleasure without responsibility. Porn is particularly sinister since it gives us pleasure without any consequence. If you have sex in real life, you'll likely have children (at some point), you have to deal with another person's feelings, and you have to consider more than just yourself. All this is part of growing up. We cannot truly grow up unless something outside ourselves is significantly important to us. That might be a child, a business, or something you are very passionate about.

Some people think it might be nice to postpone the time before they are adults, but in reality, they are missing out on what life is all about. It is possible to put off maturity without suffering an immediate penalty. The result is that the liability accrues, and it will get bigger. It is like a loan with a high interest rate that accrues into enormous compound interest. Waking up at age thirty or thirty-five and realizing you haven't yet started life as an adult is not fun. More people will experience that going forward.

Many people will wake up one day in their twenties or thirties, realizing they have wasted some of their best years playing video games, watching porn, or simply spending too much time online without going out in the real world.

Every day that you decide to go with what is convenient and easy only makes the day of reckoning much worse. By then, it might even be too late, so you spend the rest of your life lying to yourself and numbing yourself even further. It is possible to reach a point where it is so painful to admit the waste that it is practically impossible to turn things around. That is what destroys many drug addicts and alcoholics. I was frighteningly close to that point myself. I honestly believe it would have been too late if I had continued a few more years before turning things around. I would have felt that I had wasted too much time and been unable to accept the waste. I had to admit that I had wasted my early twenties before getting my internet addiction under control. Often, we have to be able to look at our situations honestly before it is possible to change. That means we must accept the waste before we are free to better ourselves.

ARROGANCE, VALIDATION, AND EGO

Using social media to validate ourselves can inflate the ego without actual accomplishments. That is more dangerous than it sounds. You can update your profile on LinkedIn to say that you are the CEO of a company that only you know exists. Whenever we receive validation for something, we reduce our drive and ambition and are prone to complacency. Many people would rather look excellent to others than actually be awesome since it requires much more work. Social media updates where we seek approval are among the biggest enemies of actual accomplishments.

We are doomed to fail when there is too much focus on talking rather than doing. On social media, the talkers rule. Showing off is rewarded online while staying under the radar and humbly working toward our goals is not rewarded. A small part of us all wants as much approval as possible with as little work as possible. This side of us is easily brought out with social media, and it requires a lot of self-control to manage it. Any creative endeavor is challenging, while talking is always easy. A good photo and "talking it up" make it easy to look like we are working on something when we actually are not doing anything. It is much easier to tweet about your upcoming book than it is to sit down and work on it.

On social media, many people make a lot of effort to portray their lives as perfect while hiding their true feelings. This only brings us further away from ourselves, making us less likely to resolve our inner issues. We have to be honest about who we are before bettering ourselves.

We need to take a step back from the constant updates and distractions online and realign with our inner vision. Caring too much about what creates the most likes on social media posts is not the way to go for real satisfaction. It is impossible to align with our true purpose while being preoccupied with our followers' thoughts about us. It is much better to stay on our path than to overly focus on social media appearances. Doing both is very difficult. There are differences among us as some people are more preoccupied with other people's feelings and thoughts. Still, we can benefit from trying to realign closer to our authentic selves.

The ego tries to convince us that everything is perfect already. It gets in our way of doing things that could improve our lives. It is hardwired into our brains, and we must constantly wrestle with it. There is a natural tendency to prefer an egoic story over actual results. It is often damaging to the ego to engage in the difficult behavior required to reach our goals. In fact, trying and potentially failing is dangerous for the ego. Why? Failing means we may have to modify our perception of ourselves. If something is holding people back from realizing their fullest potential, this might be it. To succeed, you must put your ego aside, do difficult things, and accept how this makes you feel temporarily weaker. If you stick to something for a long time, you can become competent. Competence is what breeds real confidence.

Why all this talk about ego? you might be thinking. Well, we must hold our egos back for a moment to assess our place in the world. We can only take the right action if it comes from objectivity rather than a false perception of the world. It is much easier to get closer to living aligned with your actual values if you are realistic about your starting point. That is ultimately the purpose of this book: offering tools to stop wasting time online and using the newfound time to pursue what you value most. Anton Chekhov, a renowned Russian short story writer, said, "Man will only become better when you make him see what he is like."

PERSONAL RESPONSIBILITY

If you want to cultivate digital discipline, it all starts with taking personal responsibility and removing blame. You have to realize that you are in charge of your life no matter what. Nobody cares more about your outcomes than you. Your parents, family, and boss are not in charge of your life. You are. By taking personal responsibility for yourself, you will feel more in control and realize that everything is up to you.

Society is moving in a direction where everyone is a victim, but that only makes us weaker and unhappier. Even though something might not be your fault, taking personal responsibility can help you. In *Extreme Ownership*, Jocko Willink and Leif Babin describe what it means to take personal responsibility for everything you might have the slightest impact on.[77] If we take responsibility for something that goes wrong, it makes it much easier to give feedback to people since they will let their guard down. In addition, it makes an organization work a lot better.

If you don't have a plan for your life, you will be a character in someone else's play. The path of least resistance is to spend many hours online every day on things that don't provide any real joy or value to you or others. You have to make commitments and execute them, even when it is uncomfortable. If you always follow the path of least resistance, your life will be nothing compared to what it could have been. I won't bet on your future if you cannot do inconvenient things. Nobody else should, either.

Holding ourselves accountable will remove a lot of toxicity and bitterness from our lives. If we accept that our outcomes are our responsibility, we will be motivated when we see someone doing better than ourselves at something we care about. This kind of envy can be helpful for an upward-moving individual. If we perceive our situation as undeserved and unfair, we will be more prone to passive-aggressive behavior. The moment we take personal responsibility, we become more easygoing and friendly.

BEHAVIOR MODIFICATION

To modify our behavior consistently, we need to make identity-level changes. It is not enough to rely on discipline or self-control in the long run. We need to change how we think about ourselves as well. If you consider yourself a well-trained athlete, you are much more likely to work out and eat healthily to live up to your ideal image. To make lasting changes, we have to change our underlying beliefs and cultivate discipline. Teaching someone something can be more effective in modifying our own behavior than being taught by an expert. That is because we have a strong tendency to live up to what we preach, and belief shapes behavior to a massive extent. If you consider yourself disciplined, you are likely to behave that way as well. If you teach people how to cultivate the same attribute, you are even more likely to behave how you want to.

Changing is hard because your DNA's highest priority is survival, and thriving only comes second. We are tribal animals, and as a result, we can associate danger with changing up the social hierarchy. If we go against what people expect, we experience resistance. What you have been doing until now has been sufficient for survival. Why change that when you know that it is enough to survive? If you avoid wasting time on social media, take on new habits, and improve your life, there will likely be some social resistance. People are familiar with you being a certain way, and if you try to change the status quo, they might try to resist it. Not because they are bad people, but most likely because they are uncomfortable with changes and are afraid they might lose you.

In order to change, the pain from continuing in your old patterns must be bigger than the perceived pain of changing to step up. One way to accomplish this is to put things into perspective in a different way. We do not decide to make massive changes in our lives because every day until now has been perfect. Only when we feel bad about something do we become motivated to make drastic changes. My goal with this book is to make you question your habits and how you live. Maybe you even feel a bit uncomfortable at times while reading it. If so, that is a good thing. Hopefully, you will realize it is time to become more disciplined with your digital habits.

The way to stop wasting too much time on social media will not happen by only finding clever habits and techniques. They can be useful, but to make an invisible force field that pulls you away from bad habits and distractions, you need to get a deeper perspective on life. It is a fantastic gift to live in one of the best times in human history. You are also in the privileged position to afford to spend time reading this book that you had the money to buy. You have one chance to make the most out of your time here on earth. Why not seize it and become impeccable? Why not accept a bit of discomfort here and there to strive to reach your highest aspirations and goals? When you get old, you will not remember the time you spent scrolling social media or watching YouTube videos. You will remember the challenges you overcame and your real life adventures. You will even perceive the challenging periods as better than the time wasted on distractions.

TIME MANAGEMENT AND ACCEPTING REALITY

If you cannot accept objective reality but instead try to make things rosier, you are doing yourself a big disservice. If you haven't come to terms with your mortality, you are telling yourself a fairy tale with consequences. When you deny reality because it is emotionally easier, it comes with a price. That price is procrastination, lack of clarity, and negativity.

Many people discount objectivity, refusing to experience negative emotions and learn lessons from them in the short-term. Instead, they suppress them for years and experience anxiety and depression. You can choose to run from your problems and be frustrated for the rest of your life, or you can face them and be more frustrated in the short-term before they are resolved. Then you will never have to deal with the problem again in most cases. Low-level anxieties won't stick around if you accept the harsh realities of life and expose yourself to what you fear. A good reminder to seize our opportunities instead of fearing them is a quote attributed to Confucius: "We have two lives; the second begins when we realize we only have one."

What would happen if you had to pay by the minute for your time on social media? Let's do a little thought experiment and assume it costs ten dollars an hour. Would people still end up spending 147 minutes a day on social media—the daily average in 2022? In a way, you pay more than ten dollars an hour for the time you spend passively consuming content on social media. You pay with your most precious asset: your time. Charles Darwin wrote, "A man who dares to waste one hour of time has not discovered the value of life."

If you could go back to when you were younger (or even in the recent past) and do things differently, would you? How much would you be willing to pay as an old man or woman to go back in time? I would argue that you would use everything you had and possibly everything you could borrow. We disrespect our future selves when we waste our time. If you don't value your time, you don't value your life. Seneca, the Stoic philosopher, wrote, "People are frugal in guarding their personal property; but as soon as it comes to squandering time they are most wasteful of the one thing in which it is right to be stingy."[78]

Perhaps you are considering starting an exercise routine tomorrow, but you tell yourself it is okay to wait one more day because it will be more convenient. We all do this, by the way. We think that doing something will be more convenient *in the future*. It will not. It will be even more challenging to make changes in the future because you will be older and more set in your ways. We are often delusional about the future due to our inherent optimism. The time to make changes is right now.

Perhaps you and your partner are drifting away from each other because you are afraid of being honest. Willful ignorance or constructing false beliefs for self-protection is something everyone does. I encourage you to step back and examine your patterns. Don't continue to take the easy way out. Go for the challenge. Taking the easy way out is risky; not going hard.

Brendon Burchard, a successful author and marketing trainer, attributes much of his success to gaining perspective at a young age. He was in a car accident at age nineteen and realized his mortality in this life-threatening situation. Burchard reflected on whether he had really mattered until that point in his life.[79] Obviously, we don't want to expose ourselves to life-threatening situations to realize our mortality, but running away from uncomfortable emotions only makes them persist. We should embrace life's harsh truths, and accepting them at an early age will only help us avoid time-wasting endeavors and motivate us to live with integrity—going for what we want while serving the world.

To a bigger extent, we should view our time as a commodity, just as we look at money. It is evident that time is worth more than money, but many people treat it differently. Let's say your hourly wage is twenty dollars. Now, as a thought experiment, consider every activity you do away from work in terms of dollars per hour. Would you spend your time being with friends if you had to pay twenty dollars an hour? Probably. Would you watch a boring TV series halfheartedly for three hours a day if you were charged twenty dollars an hour? No! But you might find the time to watch a genuinely interesting program. If you were charged by the hour engaging in specific activities, you would most likely find time only for the ones that provide meaning and satisfaction in your life and avoid those that drain you and don't do anything meaningful for you or others. This is how we should spend our lives. Every time we do something out of laziness or don't value our time, we are not wasting twenty dollars an hour. We are wasting something a lot more precious: potential.

You could put your time into two categories, for example. One could be things you do in the short-term to ensure a better future. Among these activities are studying, reading books, building and nurturing relationships, working out, and working on business projects. The other category could be having a genuinely enjoyable experience, like going to a fabulous party, traveling, or doing whatever you find worthwhile. The objective is to reduce the time spent on leisurely or boring activities that aren't fun or useful. If you start doing this for a period, you will find that doing a challenging and useful activity is actually more satisfying than leisurely activities. There is a barrier to entry, but we are set when we get through it. If you spend time investing in the future or in legitimately cool experiences and get rid of the rest, you will essentially optimize your life in the here and now and in the future.

Every time we delay rewards, we plant seeds that will spring into life later, giving us future satisfaction. Working out is painful initially, and reading books is not much fun if you aren't naturally inclined to it. If we stick to these habits for a month or two, they will grow on us. Suddenly, it feels enjoyable to read a book. Before you know it, it feels better to read than to scroll through social media. That is an excellent position to be in! Reading will fill your head with valuable thoughts and information that can improve your life in multiple ways. If we accept reality, knowing that the barrier to entry is uncomfortable, it is much easier to build good habits. Follow through on what you know you are supposed to do regardless of whether it is convenient.

BRAVE NEW WORLD

We live in a society where people have the option to go for instant pleasure almost all the time. In the popular novel *Brave New World*, Aldous Huxley describes a society like this. But is having it easy what gives us the most satisfaction? In George Orwell's novel *1984*, a society controlled by distributing pornography to the masses is described.[80] Huxley and Orwell had some key insights into human nature. Easy access to instant pleasure without working for it makes it more challenging to develop a good work ethic, integrity, character, or passion. The reason many people enjoy alcohol so much might be that we are reminded that we have bodies. That is easy to forget as we are becoming more sedentary and get exposed to easy pleasure all the time.

The inner qualities that make up our character and, ultimately, our internal possibility for satisfaction beyond the external bodily pleasures are what matters. Seneca wrote, "Pleasures, when they go beyond a certain limit, are but punishments." Why is this so poignant? We can easily find pleasure in an object or activity, then fail to realize that without boundaries or set limits on the time we put into it, it will control us. Balance is the key to avoiding our pleasures becoming our punishments. The body is constantly trying to balance pleasure and pain. Suppose we expose ourselves to too much easy pleasure online, for example. In that case, the body will adjust by producing uncomfortable feelings in the aftermath, such as anxiety, restlessness, or fatigue. There is a reason why many drugs, such as cocaine and ecstasy, have a comedown. When we have been exposed to too much easy pleasure, the body will adjust in the opposite direction. Pain can manifest in many ways, such as unclarity, fatigue, apathy, and much more.

Brave New World is, in many ways, a pretty accurate portrait of the world in the twentieth century,[81] which is astonishing considering that it was published in 1932. Huxley describes soma in the book as a pleasure-inducing drug with no side effects. Without it, people would start to experience their true emotions and develop a better sense of who they were. Soma soothed any conflict or uncomfortable feeling, and people relied on it to deal with everything. This drug was perhaps meant to symbolize the effect science and technology would have on us in the future. Going into a trance to escape boredom or anxiety or to induce pleasurable feelings is possible with the smartphone. Do you know anyone today who is not addicted to their smartphone? We use it for communicating, and it helps us with a lot of our daily tasks, but that doesn't explain why we check it nearly one hundred times a day on average. The reason for that is because of its drug-like component.

MICRODECISIONS

Success is won or lost in the thousands of small decisions we make every day. "Should I work on my side hustle now or do it another day?" "Do I want to experience temporary, pleasant feelings, or do I want to be productive?" These minor trade-offs between what feels best in the moment and what is best for your future will determine the amount of success in your life. Success is subjective, but this concept applies nonetheless.

You ruin your future when you choose the convenient option rather than what you should have been doing. When you decide to relax for two more minutes before beginning the project, then add on a break for a couple of minutes, this is where you fail. Success is won or lost in the accumulation of those small decisions, and if you manage to get a slightly larger fraction of them right every day, you will become successful fast. Having the internal control to dive into tasks and situations you can easily postpone is a fantastic ability.

You get to vote thousands of times daily on how your future will turn out. Vote with your future in mind, not with what is convenient right now. Most people do not want to hear this. This is the shortcut if there ever existed one. If you stick to something longer and care less about your short-term emotions, you will become more effective than most. Pretty soon, your body and mind will adapt, and you will have set a new and higher standard for yourself that enables you to work harder and make more reasonable decisions with less effort. Your competition is preoccupied with doing what's convenient, most likely checking social media or watching cat videos. If you adopt this future-oriented behavior pattern, you will be well on your way to success, whatever that means for you.

Remember, change requires us to strengthen desirable pathways in our brain while weakening undesirable ones. We can reinforce good pathways by choosing to take action, no matter how small the decision.

THE EIGHTH WONDER OF THE WORLD

Good habits and actions repeated over time can lead to great results. It works like a snowball rolling down a hill. It might be a tiny snowball, but it accumulates more snow and gets bigger as it accelerates. When it finally settles, it can be huge. Starting out cultivating digital discipline can look pretty much the same. When we carve out more time to do something else, we will build self-control and have more time to focus on something useful, like working out, being with friends, or working on a project. You can implement new habits, such as going for a walk thirty minutes a day instead of scrolling through your social media feeds. These small habits rewire your neurochemistry. When you build discipline, a small new habit can cascade into a myriad of other good things. A few years later, the seemingly minute decision to abandon the phone for thirty minutes a day to get some fresh air might be the catalyst for a completely different life if you maintain the momentum.

The seemingly inconsequential choices we make every day have the most significant long-term impact. What are you doing when no one else is watching? Are you slacking off or doing something that will help your life long-term? Are you engaging in destructive habits or doing your best to carve out a better life? In many cases, it is enough to desire to improve one's circumstances. With time, you will learn valuable things, and you will have more self-control and discipline if you stick to it.

What would you spend your time on if you had a couple of extra hours daily? Do you want to start working out or start a business? Massive changes can happen pretty quickly if you free up two hours every day that used to be wasted online. Let's say you found the time to work out for one hour every day and spend one hour with friends building relationships. One month in, the changes might not be that noticeable, but your energy levels would probably have started going up, and you would notice some minor changes in your happiness and health. After one year, you will probably have more energy to tackle other things. Perhaps you got promoted because you had more energy to focus on work. A few years later, the extra pay could give you the chance to take a year off work to start a business or follow a different passion. If you free up a little time every day away from digital use, your life could change drastically for the better. Habits are formed by the principle of compound interest: tiny habits that seem unnoticeable in the moment stack up over time and have significant consequences—good or bad.

Our psyche is not good at seeing how small behavioral changes affect the bigger picture. It might seem pointless if we reduce screen time every day for one week and replace it with something else; your lifestyle would pretty much be the same one week later. Unless we lengthen the time span, we will be stuck right where we are. Don't give up when trying to make changes. Remind yourself to look further into the future and shift your time perspective. The payout comes later, but it is worth it.

We tend to discount future rewards and find (temporary) comfort in instant payoffs. But if we learn to hold off on immediate gratification and live more with the future in mind, we are almost guaranteed happiness and increased well-being. The only trade-off is that you can't have as much pleasure *right now*. Remember, though, that our habits are affected by compound interest. Go to the gym even on days when it is inconvenient. Do what you are supposed to do. Take on new habits regardless of the short-term consequence. Let compound interest take care of the rest. Your future self will thank you for it.

EXERCISES

- Can you think of situations where you changed a small thing in your life, and it made a big difference later?
- Picture yourself three or five years into the future. Where do you want to be? Imagine this version of you as vividly as possible. What is something that your future self would be grateful for you accomplishing today? When we start becoming more conscious about our future selves, we are more likely to build habits today that will make us happier in the future.

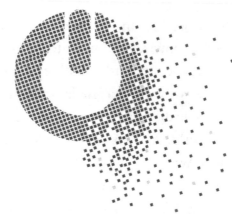

CHAPTER 7

FINDING PURPOSE

*If you don't make the time to work on creating the life
that you want, you're eventually going to be forced to
spend a lot of time dealing with a life you don't want.*
—Kevin Ngo

Our outcomes in life largely come down to our habits and the goals that fuel them. We need to know where we are going. Otherwise, we are leaving our future up to chance. This chapter will help you realize how you should spend your time. If you already have specific goals or a purpose in life, that is great. When we have a purpose, we can take on habits that will get us closer to where we want to go. Knowing what you want is the foundation for building your life. In the following chapters, the goal is to implement the knowledge from part 1 to make a lasting change.

The brain subconsciously modifies our behavior to reach our goals. Before we write our goals down, they are merely fairy dust—intangible thoughts that have not been assigned a concrete form in the world. When we put them on paper, they materialize in our brains. What we observe travels to the brain's hippocampus for analysis. This is called *encoding*, and writing something down improves the encoding process.[82]

When we have set goals for ourselves, we should change our focus from the outcome to the process. Athletes prepare for a competition by focusing on a system and daily decisions. Focusing on the process rather than only living with the future in mind makes reaching our goals way more effective and enjoyable. Of course, we need to be conscious of where we want to go, but once we know, the focus should be on the small, daily habits that could take us there.

We need goals that match our deepest aspirations in order to have bulletproof motivation. What we think we want at the surface level will always lose out to our identity-level goals and motivation in the long run. For instance, if you set a New Year's resolution to work out three times a week, but your identity is that of a lazy person, it will be almost impossible to stick to the new habit. On the other hand, our actions change us as well. When you show up at the gym, you reinforce an identity as a healthy and athletic person. It works both ways.

Some people think that having good habits and being disciplined restricts freedom. That is far from the truth. If you are willing to be disciplined, you will have freedom later. For example, if you are disciplined with how you use money and save more than you spend, you are on your way to financial freedom. As you know, discipline leads to freedom. It can be rewarding to suppress impulses as long as it helps us reach our long-term goals.

Having a purpose is one of our most fundamental needs. It is crucial for our well-being, and without it we suffer psychologically. People who lack clarity and purpose are vulnerable to anxiety and depression. Purpose directs and motivates us. If we lack something important to focus on, it is very easy to end up looking at social media for hours or watching people copulating online instead. Having no purpose opens the doors to many mental issues. The brilliant psychiatrist and Holocaust survivor Viktor Frankl captures the essence of purpose: "What man actually needs is not a tensionless state but rather the striving and struggling for some goal worthy of him."[83]

How can you achieve something if you don't know where to put in work? You can easily spot someone living in alignment with their purpose by seeing if they have zest and sharp eyes. We can also determine when someone has lost track of their purpose. In the same way we can see it in others, we can also notice this within ourselves. Living in alignment with our purpose makes us feel excited and gives us a sense of flow. On the other hand, you can notice yourself drifting away from your purpose when you accomplish something and feel no pleasure. You will know it deep down. Fortunately, we can continuously tap into our purpose and get going again.

Who are you, and what do you want out of life? You have to answer these two questions to be committed to your path.

Reflect on them. Listen to your intuition and try new things. Eventually, you will know with whom and how you should spend your time. That requires attentiveness and being undistracted. Distracting ourselves is the price we pay for not having a purpose. If you want to accomplish something, you won't have time to waste online. I can't stress this enough: if you lack a purpose and have nothing to strive for, you will become prone to anxiety, depression, and endless distractions. If you don't know what you want, you have to take on challenges to get closer to finding your true self and determining what you want to accomplish.

David Deida wrote about purpose and integrity in his book *The Way of the Superior Man*: "Everything in your life, from your diet to your career, must be aligned with your purpose if you are to act with coherence and integrity in the world. If you know your purpose, your deepest desire, then the secret of success is to discipline your life so that you support your deepest purpose and minimize distractions and detours."[84]

It is common for people to expect something different from us than what we want to do deep down. In these situations, you need to follow your vision. You will be motivated in a totally different way if you are doing something because *you* want to rather than doing what other people expect from you.

PRIORITIZATION

The ability to prioritize and make sacrifices is crucial for reaching goals. Should you prioritize catching up with friends or working on that business project? We constantly have to make these kinds of decisions. The most important thing we can do to gain time for our priorities is eliminate the time we spend on meaningless distractions. Let's do some math to illustrate.

We all have 168 hours a week at our disposal. Let's assume you sleep eight hours a day. That leaves you with 112 hours. Next, let's assume you spend forty hours a week at work. Now you have seventy-two hours left. Wouldn't you be able to find a lot of quality time with friends and family, working out, and working on a business project if you wanted to? Of course, you could. You would just have to eliminate most distractions and be disciplined with how you spend your time. Some people will say that they don't have the energy to be so disciplined. Many people think they need to watch TV to relax after work. We all need to recharge, but this time should be spent on something that invigorates us.

A lot of the things we think refresh us actually sap our energy. You get depleted when you choose to watch TV instead of relaxing by walking or taking a nap. In addition, it is easy to waste more time than necessary when we try to recharge while consuming digital content. When we cut toxic activities from our life, we get much more energy.

The legendary investor Warren Buffett shared an exercise with an employee that shows the importance of prioritization. Buffett told him to write down his top twenty-five goals in life and then focus on only the top five.[85] I am not necessarily saying you should live this way, but we get in trouble when we try to do too much simultaneously. An easy way to gain more energy and time for what you value is to significantly cut down your time spent on digital distractions.

At the end of the day, if you want to have several good things in your life, you will have to say no to something. If you want to have a great relationship with your family and spend quality time with them, excel at work, stay in great shape, and read many books, it is doable—but it requires making sacrifices. You will not have the time to waste hours per day on social media. Too much digital use comes at the expense of other things that would have provided more satisfaction in your life. You need to be disciplined if you care about your family, work, and other priorities. Otherwise, you won't allocate your time as you should, and your future happiness will suffer. The happiness of those around you will be undermined as well. It is your responsibility to become the best version of yourself for the sake of the people around you.

With discipline and purpose, it is possible to change the world. Mahatma Gandhi opposed the British rule of India and made it his life's mission to achieve Indian independence. He believed strongly in self-discipline, and he frequently tested his will. For example, he fasted for twenty-one days to heal Hindu-Muslim relations. Gandhi was prepared to forgo his basic needs to achieve his bigger goals. He also believed that we should focus on improving ourselves instead of others because we have control of our actions, not others' actions. Gandhi's nonviolent opposition had an enormous impact, showing what can be achieved when purpose and immense willpower are combined.

At the end of the day, the only sustainable way to take permanent control of our digital life is to set clear goals and priorities. If you want to accomplish something and know that scrolling on social media will take you further from your goal, putting the phone away will become more effortless. This goal will be different for everyone, and it will change with time as well. For instance, some people's main priority is to be the best parents they can be. Others want to be professional athletes, excel at a craft, or succeed in their careers. Whatever you want to accomplish, having a goal makes you much more likely to say no to the things that don't matter or that hurt you in the long-term.

EXERCISES

- Reflect on what you want out of life and who you should surround yourself with. What lifestyle do you ideally envision for yourself? Do you have a burning desire to achieve something? Who would you have to surround yourself with to achieve those goals? What satisfies you most in life? Perhaps spending time with your family or your career gives you the most satisfaction. Reflect on your passions, your goals, and who you should spend your time with. What makes you truly excited in life and sparks your curiosity and enthusiasm?

- With your purpose now defined, you can begin to set goals that align with that purpose. Make a list of short-term, medium-term, and long-term goals, then decide what small steps you can take now to start tackling those goals. When goals are set, you can build systems to help you stay accountable.

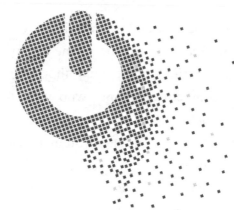

CHAPTER 8

HOW TO BUILD SELF-CONTROL

The reason it's important to push hardest when you want to quit the most is because it helps you callous your mind. It's the same reason why you have to do your best work when you are the least motivated.
—David Goggins

One attribute has special importance because of all the noise and distractions we encounter every day in the twenty-first century: self-control. Self-control is the bedrock for any other good attribute. We will lose a lot of time and fail to commit to our deepest desires and dreams if we can't control ourselves. People are free to spend their time in any way they want, and most aren't serious about how they expend it. That is good news for competitive people who want to achieve something but unfortunate for the ones struggling. We need purpose and self-control to direct our attention in a meaningful way. Purpose directs us, and self-control makes sure that we stay on track.

Ernest Shackleton was an Irish explorer who led three expeditions to Antarctica in the early 1900s. He also understood practical psychology incredibly well and embodied unbelievable mental strength. During the Imperial Trans-Antarctic Expedition from 1914 to 1917, he and his men tried to cross the entire continent of Antarctica. Unfortunately, their ship, *Endurance*, froze into an ice floe and sank, resulting in them being stranded on the ice off the Antarctic continent. With only a few small boats from the ship to carry them to safety, Shackleton was determined to make every effort to survive. They were more than a thousand kilometers from the closest inhabited island, so they had to cross some of the harshest open-water passages in the world.

Shackleton managed to keep his men from despair by using his excellent psychological understanding and discipline. They were stranded for months on an ice floe before abandoning it to make the trip to the uninhabited Elephant Island. Shackleton and a few of his men embarked on one of the most challenging open-boat journeys of all time. They sailed in an open boat only twenty-two feet long, traveled eight hundred miles, and eventually managed to reach South Georgia, where they were saved. Afterward, they returned and saved the men they had to leave on Elephant Island. In the end, everyone survived the expedition.

During the hardship that lasted more than one year, Shackleton never complained or showed any sign of weakness. The men were constantly hungry and cold due to minimal variation in the food they ate and the extremely harsh climate of Antarctica, but Shackleton's steadfast optimism and discipline prevented the other men from sinking into despair. Shackleton realized they would likely die, but he remained positive nonetheless.[86] If someone can remain positive and solution oriented in those circumstances, so can we in our modern lives.

People used to value discipline more back in the day than we do now. Most people nowadays want to take it easy and avoid difficult challenges by following the path of least resistance. To become really disciplined, though, we have to do things that are not always the easiest option and take full ownership of our lives. Willpower is about exerting our will to accomplish something, and it involves focusing all our attention on achieving a goal. Self-control is about controlling our impulses. It could be viewed as our ability to regulate ourselves and resist actions against our priorities.

Self-control and willpower go hand in hand. We must be firm in saying no to the behaviors that will weaken our resolve. Clear priorities and a sense of direction help support us in our weak moments. Self-control works like a muscle—if we train it, we will get stronger. That is why it is healthy to keep the body a bit stressed: our bodies and minds will weaken if we remain idle and never challenge ourselves.

A study on Turkish men found that alcohol-dependent people who viewed themselves as powerless were more likely to drink again.[87] The researchers found that our beliefs about recovery play a big role in whether we modify our behavior or not. This illustrates that the way we look at ourselves shapes our behavior, so we need to be aware of the stories we tell ourselves and ideally change them to something that empowers us. We have a lot more endurance and power than we think. It is all about controlling the mind. Our thoughts about whether we are powerless or powerful are crucial. If you think of yourself as helpless, you will essentially become powerless, and vice versa.

You can build self-esteem by following through on your commitments. If you honor the promises you make to yourself, you will live with integrity. You will build self-esteem by going the extra mile and continually honoring your word to yourself and others. People will trust you because of your track record if you do this. That is a great position to be in.

Making small commitments and following through on them every day, regardless of whether you feel like it, will also increase your mental toughness. This doesn't have to include monumental tasks, but simply doing what you have promised yourself will skyrocket your confidence and increase your mental strength. Aside from becoming more trustworthy, you will gain a more positive outlook on life. Your hesitation and uncertainty will be gone, and your mood will improve. Gradually, you will start seeing life differently when you experience the positive effects of always honoring your words. It will not always be convenient to do this, but that is why it builds mental strength.

David Goggins, an endurance athlete, motivational speaker, author, and former Navy SEAL, is often considered the toughest man alive. Goggins is notorious for his mental strength and shares ways to become mentally tough in his book *Can't Hurt*

Me. He believes that suffering is necessary to grow and that the key is diving into what we find uncomfortable and gradually taking on greater challenges.[88]

Callusing our minds is about pushing against our limitations—including things we are not motivated by—and growing as a result. Most of us dislike chores, but in reality, they are an opportunity to test and build our mental strength. Every time we have to do something undesirable, it is actually an excellent opportunity to strengthen ourselves. Eventually, you can move on to more challenging tasks as well. That is how business success happens too. According to Brian Tracy, author and motivational speaker, your reward for overcoming your current life obstacles is bigger and more complex challenges. Start becoming aware when you have to do something but don't really feel like doing it. That is your chance to work on yourself.

It is almost like we detoxify our brains when we challenge ourselves with something difficult and overcome it. To overcome physical or mental challenges, we are forced to think positively. Otherwise, we would give up. If you go for a run, you might think about winding down and walking, for example. Every time you avoid listening to those thoughts and run farther, you are priming your mind to become more positive as you stop acting on negative or limiting thoughts.

If we have nothing going on, the mind tends to create problems. You must choose your obstacles by taking on responsibility; otherwise, your brain will create its problems. Exerting our will to accomplish something daily is the best remedy for maintaining a positive and well-functioning mind. If you move toward pain, it becomes less significant. When you run from it, it chases after you and grows.

Self-discipline takes a lot of effort out of the equation. If we become disciplined, we have to expend less willpower or self-control on our daily choices. It takes decision fatigue out of the question. It will become much easier if we remove the option not to do something. We might as well just do what we planned in the best mood possible since we have no other choice. Will-power and self-control can wane, while discipline is constant. You either go to the gym every day at 5:00 p.m. or you don't.

WHAT WILL HAPPEN IN THE FUTURE?

We have experienced enormous technological advancements in the last few years. Graphics are improving, and new apps are even better at capturing our attention. The stimuli we encounter with the digital tools we use are already so captivating that most people spend a few hours online daily on unnecessary activities. Some people could argue that this is fulfilling them. As you now know, however, it is really about quick and easy dopamine hits that are evolutionarily relevant but only sap our energy. When marketers become better at capturing our attention, when graphics are better, and when virtual reality makes another giant leap, we might end up in a place where very few people can withstand the stimuli.

Many people have already lost complete control of how they spend their time online. People who are disciplined and conscious in this area will fare much better. Luckily, we are always free to change if we want to. When lying on the couch with nothing to do, we sometimes need to flex our self-control muscles to get up and do something rather than scrolling through social media.

BUILDING MENTAL STRENGTH TO COMBAT BOREDOM

In chapter 6, I mentioned that it is much easier to get by in the Western world than ever before. We can order food and have it delivered to our door. We can take the bus or drive everywhere we want. We can watch a YouTube video instead of reading. We have warm water in the shower in seconds. A few generations back, it was common for families to lose children at an early age to illness or accidents, and people had to work grueling, long days doing manual labor. Farmers, for instance, had no option but to work hard. Because it was tough to survive, people had to become mentally strong to get through their everyday lives.

Without all these obstacles today, we have a lot of free time on our hands. Instead of filling it with productive activities, we go for easy, instant gratification online. We always have access to entertainment and stimuli online to minimize our boredom. But to build mental strength, we have to impose challenges on ourselves that aren't necessary. If we lack enough motivation, we will not have the leverage to put ourselves through adversity.

Not allowing this easy pleasure thoughtlessly is vital, as it will ruin your capacity to experience joy and excitement. It will only dull you to real, deeper emotions. Say no to the impulse to pick up the phone every time you are bored. Allow yourself to be bored for a while. Before you know it, you will become more grounded and can derive pleasure from simpler things, like playing board games, reading a book, painting, or writing. These things will only be boring if we constantly engage in compulsive overconsumption. Develop your self-control and say no to constant stimuli. You will be well rewarded.

BUILDING SELF-CONTROL

Self-control is a trainable attribute. If you go to the gym, you will eventually get stronger but will initially be taxed after a hard training session. You must gradually build your mental strength, and before you know it, things that used to be difficult will seem effortless. Once you have developed some "mental" muscle, you can go at it harder again and build it even further. A few months later (or a couple of years later), your life can be very different, in a good way.

We are all mental athletes, whether we realize it or not. How well you do in life comes down to how good of a mental athlete you are. Do you use mental energy on things out of your control or on the things you can potentially influence? Do you spend much time in unproductive emotional states, or do you turn things around rapidly? In fact, how much time you spend in resourceful emotional states determines the quality of your life and how successful you will become. If you take on many challenging projects and have a fulfilling but busy schedule, you will have no other choice than to be in resourceful emotional states most of the time.

When things get difficult, you will have the time to shine. That is an excellent opportunity to show your brilliance and grit, to work on your self-discipline, grow, and get stronger. Reprogramming your brain to look at everything as a challenge is possible—and necessary to thrive.

Procrastination is the worst enemy of inner peace and well-being. When we condition ourselves to do what we know to be right and avoid doing what's convenient, our internal well-being will increase tremendously. When our mental strength increases, we will dive into tasks head-on much more effortlessly. Roman emperor Marcus Aurelius had an impactful directive: "Be tolerant with others and strict with yourself."

WAYS TO DEVELOP YOUR MENTAL STRENGTH

Here are some practical ways to start building self-control and develop your mental strength:

- Take cold showers. Not only is this an excellent way to work on your discipline, but research points toward several health benefits.[89]
- Tackle your weaknesses head-on and try to resolve them. This will make you a more well-rounded person and better equipped to handle what life throws at you.
- Establish a morning routine and follow it religiously every day. It doesn't have to be hard, but this immediately sets the tone for the rest of the day.
- Change your perception of what is possible. Do you think it is hard to go for a run for an hour? If you were in the wilderness trying to survive, you could go for days and maybe weeks without food. Considering this, does it seem so difficult to get in a morning run?
- Practice honesty. It is not easy to always be honest, but it will help make life easier and enable you to become more disciplined. The prefrontal cortex is involved when we tell the truth, which can sometimes be uncomfortable, indicating that it requires willpower.

- Keep your promises to yourself and others, even when it is inconvenient. Make sure to go to the gym if you have told yourself, you would do so. Help your friend with moving even if you are tired. Fulfilling your commitments goes a long way in building self-discipline.

We are all mental athletes, whether we want to be or not. Remember that every time we challenge ourselves a bit further, we move the needle a little bit and become even stronger. Stretch your comfort zone to experience more self-esteem and a greater sense of accomplishment, which will cascade into a myriad of other benefits.

EXERCISES

- Make a point of always keeping the promises you make to yourself and others.
- Do something that challenges you regularly. For example, work out and push it a bit further than what you are used to.

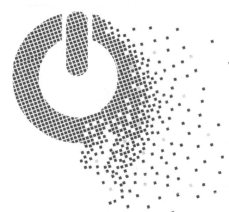

CHAPTER 9

REBUILDING YOUR ABILITY TO FOCUS

*Concentrate every minute like a Roman—like a man—
on doing what's in front of you with precise and genuine
seriousness, tenderly, willingly, with justice. And on
freeing yourself from all other distractions.*
—Marcus Aurelius

O ne of the biggest challenges of our time is staying focused amidst temptations and distractions. We all have a personal Times Square with bright lights and shiny apps in our pockets. Everything is gamified to capture our attention, and it is a huge industry. We need to be used to not having constant access to dopamine if we want to reestablish a long attention span. Many successful people say their attention span was the deciding factor in their success.

Focus can be defined as our ability to concentrate on or pay particular attention to something. This ability is closely linked to self-control. We basically need to have control of ourselves to be able to control our attention.

Our attention is the product in a lot of places these days. That means the number of eyeballs on something is what determines revenue. A few years ago, the most intruding commercials used to be on TV and in magazines. Today, everyone can compete for your attention on a device we use for everything. Our smartphones are incredibly ingrained in our daily lives. We use them when making payments, ordering food, talking to people, reading, and much more. When we do something out of necessity on our phone, like paying a bill, it is extremely easy to do something unproductive as well. In the beginning, if we want to use our phones in a more disciplined way, we need to barrel through some discomfort.

We have the option to go down two different paths:

- We can realize the importance of maintaining our ability to focus and practice digital discipline.
- We can take the path of least resistance and live a life of easy, online pleasure that progressively worsens.

Our relationship with digital devices is pretty much our relationship with life itself. If you constantly allow yourself online stimuli, it is much easier to go for a Snickers instead of a salad at the supermarket. If you have a plan and a purpose in life, you won't find as much time for distractions online and will be more disciplined. It all comes down to whether we choose instant gratification or delayed gratification. If you are disciplined online, you are training yourself to be disciplined in real life as well.

If you can't tolerate boredom, you won't have the ability to focus deeply either. Being intensely focused is almost impossible without being present. Even if you schedule time for focused work, working effectively will be nearly impossible if you never withstand boredom at other times during the day. If you can't avoid glancing at your smartphone while waiting in line at the coffee shop, you will not be able to focus intensely on work. Concentration requires the ability to withstand temptations. Otherwise, we will start checking our phones every five minutes on autopilot. It can be nice to have some periods every day where you are completely offline. That allows your brain some time to get used to not being constantly connected with the noise from your smartphone.

Walking to work can be an excellent chance to listen to your favorite podcast or music, but sometimes it is better to have no digital stimuli. Silent moments allow us to be present and provide a window to avoid digitally elevated dopamine levels. Concentrating on a task at work is usually not very stimulating, and we need to get used to such low-stimuli activities to lock in fully later. That will allow you to get more meaningful work done.

With too many temptations and shiny objects around us, our focus suffers. When there is too much of something, it typically creates a lack of something else. Basic economic theory says that as something gets scarcer, its value increases. That means that if you build the ability to focus deeply, you are well positioned to thrive in the economy.

To maintain our ability to focus well, we need to be conscious of several things. We need to tolerate boredom and not let our devices constantly interrupt us. Sleeping well and having a good diet will also affect how well we can focus, as will resolving emotional problems. If you live healthily, stay connected to people, and allow time every day away from digital notifications and interruptions, you are in a great position to enjoy life more fully and be successful in your endeavors.

Many successful people believe their ability to do single-minded tasks for long periods was the foundation for their success. Bill Gates and Warren Buffett are two such people. Gates spent his time in his youth becoming an expert programmer. Buffett has spent his life reading financial statements and keeping an enormous web of information in his head about the economy and different companies. Gates and Buffett have spent tremendous amounts of time focusing single-mindedly without distractions on the phone or from something else. Nor can we expect success by being glued to our devices. Having a good attention span is fundamental when learning any skill set.

To feel alive and vibrant, we need to focus on what is happening right before us. Our only access to life is in the fleeting moments. If we constantly think about the future or the past and remain unable to be present in the moment, we not only lose out on life, but our finances will suffer, our relationships will suffer, and our overall well-being will suffer. To stay present, we have to control our attention.

Albert Einstein was a mediocre student when he was a teenager, but he was so immersed in his work on relativity that he made world-changing contributions to science. In order to single-mindedly focus on his theories, he didn't pay attention to anything else. Carl Jung had his study tower where he would retreat to work on his ideas on psychology. Many great thinkers prefer solitude when working on their crafts. We have to close the door, sit there, and just think to solve complex problems. Uninterrupted. That cannot happen with a phone close by pinging and ringing every five minutes. Or worse, if we feel compelled to check it as soon as we feel a hint of boredom. To do great, meaningful work, we must allow ourselves to drill down deeply into a problem, sometimes for hours without interruption. In the quiet of going for a walk, working out, or hiking without interruptions, we make connections between things. Our creativity is sparked when our mind is allowed to wander a bit, and we haven't bombarded it with endless stimuli. As Steve Jobs said: "Creativity is just connecting things." We need time without distractions to allow our brains to connect meaningful things.

DISTRACTIONS AT WORK

There is a limit to how quickly we can absorb information. If we get exposed to more information faster, we learn less. If you deal with email and phone calls all day, you will be constantly interrupted and never reach peak concentration. Many office workers today also communicate with an internal messaging app. The result is that workers end up in a frenetic blur of distractions until the day ends. By that point, they feel mentally depleted. It is not easy to shift gears, sit down with a book, and relax after a day like that.

If you work in an environment like this, turning off notifications now and then is important to allow time for deep work, at least in the short-term. The long-term solution might be finding a job that makes it easier to prioritize deep work and doesn't require you to be available 24/7. If you work in an environment with endless messages, emails, phone calls, and meetings, cultivating digital discipline will be a lot harder in your spare time. To combat this and give yourself freedom to focus more deeply at work, start by turning off notifications as much as possible, and allow at least an hour or two every day when you are unavailable during office hours.

FOCUS AND EMOTIONAL REGULATION

Our ability to focus depends on different brain regions, and it has synergies with other cognitive abilities. For example, becoming skillful at focusing your attention can also help you control your emotions. Attentional regulation can be trained with practice, which is a vital part of emotional regulation.[90] That means that if we manage to be more conscious of how we direct our attention, we can become happier and experience more positive emotions. Then we can avoid dwelling on negative emotions and focus on the positives instead. That requires mindfulness, and if we lose control of our attention many times a day online, it will be more difficult to direct our attention differently when we are experiencing negative emotions as well.

Some people claim that happiness is simply the absence of negative emotions. Considering that focusing well helps us regulate emotions, it becomes clear how social media use can negatively affect our psyche. If something damages our ability to focus, it will also harm our ability to regulate emotions—no wonder depression and anxiety are skyrocketing among teens.

Meditation is very effective at increasing our emotional well-being and countering all the distractions around us. Meditation is about recognizing the self and observing thoughts drift by. It is a great way to combat negativity, slow racing thoughts, and calm yourself. Mindfulness meditation, which combines focusing on the breath and mind awareness, can be a good daily practice. Ten minutes a day of meditation can go a long way to start observing our thoughts and not identifying with them. Taking a time-out every day with meditation makes it much easier to pause when you feel an impulse to check your smartphone.

DOPAMINE SENSITIVITY AND THE ABILITY TO WORK HARD

If you increase your dopamine sensitivity, you will be able to work harder and enjoy it more. You will get more excited about your daily habits, and things will feel more satisfying.

People with higher dopamine levels in a region of the brain called the caudate nucleus focus more on the payoff of a task than how difficult it seems. This means they can work harder than others since they are sensitive to the reward on the other end.[91] There are many ways to increase our dopamine sensitivity. Part of it is about avoiding too much time spent on harmful activities. Moderating internet usage, avoiding junk food, avoiding porn, and living a healthy lifestyle are all beneficial.

FLOW AND PRESENCE

Flow is a state where we lose track of time because we are fully absorbed in a task. We need several minutes of total concentration to reach a flow state, and when we do, it is blissful. Unfortunately, distractions as brief as 2.8 seconds can break up a flow state.[92] Our brains have become accustomed to being interrupted constantly. We constantly shift gears to answer emails, check Snapchat, or answer messages. That starkly contrasts with the deep attention we need to thrive academically or professionally.

If we constantly ruminate, our ability to perform at anything will suffer. When we are present, we become more effective communicators, connect more easily with others, and get closer to being the best version of ourselves. The smartphone's mere presence can reduce our ability to be fully immersed in our daily lives. On some level, we are aware that the virtual world is easily accessible. Peak experiences and meaningful work require our minds' undivided attention. Former US president Bill Clinton mastered this ability. He gave everyone he met his full attention, which garnered likability. Clinton would make you feel like you were the only person in the room when he talked to you.[93] Having that kind of presence is possible only if you are fully immersed in what is happening in front of you.

A survey by Matthew A. Killingsworth and Daniel T. Gilbert of Harvard University looked into presence and how often we think about something different from what we are doing. A staggering 47 percent of the time, people think about something different from what they are doing. Having drifting thoughts is the default way our brains operate. When we are present, we are happier, though. What we think while doing something is more important for our happiness than what we do.[94] This means that our interpretation matters much more than what happens to us.

FOCUS: AN ECONOMIC ADVANTAGE

Technology is racing forward, and we see big disruptions in many fields. The workforce is competing globally for many positions. Globalization has made us a lot more connected, and people from all over the world can compete for the same jobs in fields such as IT. We are getting more specialized, and deeper knowledge within an area is becoming more sought after as nearly every profession accelerates the skills and knowledge required to do the work.

To thrive in this environment, we need the ability now more than ever to focus single-mindedly on a task for a long time—a skill that will probably become even scarcer. Expertise in a field sets us apart—we will get paid well if we are among the best in our niche. Thus, we must update our skills and drill deep into our subjects of interest to stay relevant. This especially applies to highly skilled professions where people have started working with AI tools such as ChatGPT. Hopefully, we can work with these tools rather than get replaced by them, but on the flip side, this means that we must constantly update our skills to stay relevant.

There are several online platforms that can help us focus better. I often use Focusmate, a virtual coworking platform that partners you with someone for twenty-five, fifty, or seventy-five minutes to help you both work uninterrupted. This live accountability makes it easier for me to focus. It also allows you to take breaks between sessions. Focusmate is a positive example of tech being used to enhance our lives, and hopefully, more platforms like it will emerge.

The internet can be a fantastic resource for improving work productivity, staying connected to people, and providing an enormous vault of information, or it can be a source of hedonistic pleasure. People who use the internet in a disciplined way to access the information they need and avoid harmful content will mainly experience the benefits. A few years later, the knowledge accumulated from spending our time wisely online can be extraordinarily valuable.

On the other hand, people who don't have control of their attention and follow the shiny or trendy thing online will temporarily experience some positive stimulation but have very little to show off. As you know, too much passive consumption online will result in losing out on knowledge, real-world experience, and deeper social relationships. Being disciplined with our attention will be a superpower in the twenty-first century.

BLOOM'S TAXONOMY

Overuse of meaningless digital content affects our comprehension. We can determine to what extent using Bloom's taxonomy, an ordering of skills that details the different levels of understanding. Since we tend to scan short texts these days and then move on, we can lose out on the work required to understand something deeply. This was true for me a few years back when I would skim or avoid long paragraphs in short newspaper articles since it was too challenging for me to thoroughly read them.

Bloom's taxonomy has six levels:

1. Remembering facts.
2. Understanding facts.
3. Solving problems in new scenarios by applying knowledge.
4. Analyzing and seeing how specific information relates to other things.
5. Evaluating the validity of ideas.
6. Producing a unique communication by putting parts together as a whole.[95]

According to Bloom's model, if we can only remember facts or recognize something, we do not know that subject well. To have useful knowledge, we need to understand how to apply information in a new context.

Many aspiring entrepreneurs go to seminars or read books about success. This kind of knowledge has value when we realize how to apply it to our circumstances. Recollection of facts doesn't help us before we see the connections the facts have to our lives. Learning, analyzing, and evaluating requires focus. If you want to understand something at a deep level, you must give it your undivided attention. When we get too distracted by the internet and the constant use of our cell phones, the self-control and mental RAM necessary to internalize concepts and make thought-out arguments are gone. It is much easier to have a sufficient attention span to excel in medical school or an engineering job if you avoid overstimulating yourself with TikTok, Instagram, and porn.

EXERCISES

- Have you noticed a difference in your ability to focus since you began using a smartphone? How old were you when this technology entered your life? Can you notice a difference in how well you can zone in and focus on something in periods where you use your phone less and in periods where you use it more?
- Prioritize and make time for work without distractions. Simply practicing the ability to focus single-mindedly will aid you in all endeavors.

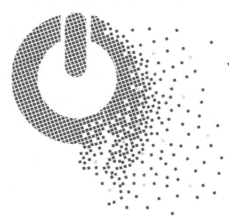

CHAPTER 10

DIGITAL DISCIPLINE: MAKE LASTING CHANGES

How long are you going to wait before you demand the best for yourself?
—Epictetus

U ntil now, we have gone through why we should change our digital habits and underlying thoughts and philosophies that can help us achieve that. Let's implement some habits to ensure lasting changes. So how do we go from wasting time every day online to building a new lifestyle centered on offline activities or digital activities that can give us long-term value, such as reading, spending more time with loved ones, creating content, or building a business? There will be some lonely moments when you decide to create this new lifestyle. But in the end, you will be tremendously thankful to yourself when you have great things to look back on that wouldn't have come your way otherwise.

Growth is not always pleasurable; it involves challenges and listening to inner music that can sometimes be uncomfortable. Pain and discomfort are the best motivators there are. When we suppress uncomfortable feelings or boredom by scrolling, we ruin our natural chance to build motivation and change our circumstances.

Things will be hard in the beginning if you make drastic changes. That is how it is and should be. When I chose to stop using my phone or computer after 10:00 p.m., I fell asleep most nights around 1:00 a.m. Initially, I had to go through many uncomfortable emotional experiences that I had suppressed for years. I felt lonely, but it got a lot better after a while. I found alternative ways to deal with the emotions and felt compelled to spend more time with other people.

Many habits and techniques that can help us avoid distractions will be covered in this chapter. Sometimes we cannot fix the root cause without first implementing some clever techniques. In addition, establishing good daily routines makes it much easier to stay disciplined. The difference between good and bad circumstances in your life is just the accumulated difference between good or bad habits repeated for years. We are what we repeatedly do, and the quality of our habits determines the quality of our lives. Author Will

Durant echoes this sentiment: "Excellence, then, is not an act, but a habit."

If your favorite cookies are on the kitchen table, you must resist temptation every time you pass them. That requires a lot of self-control. Having constant access to something that triggers cravings makes it much more likely in the short-term that you will relapse and eat something you shouldn't. On the other hand, if you never resist temptations and suddenly come over for some delicious cookies at a friend's house, you will eat more than you should. That is because you haven't flexed your self-control muscles for a while. To remain strong mentally, we need to get through tough challenges regularly.

REPLACING ACTIVITIES AND BUILDING NEW HABITS

When we start limiting screen time, a void can quickly arise. To experience lasting change, we need to fill this void with new activities such as reading or playing an instrument. They require no planning and can be done immediately when we get bored. These kinds of activities are ideal replacements for scrolling on the phone or surfing the internet. Since we tend to pull out our smartphones whenever we get bored, we need to build an alternative habit. If you feel like being social, you can call a friend and plan something. Pick up a long-term project like writing a book or learning to play the guitar. Find something more meaningful to replace downtime by yourself.

We can't remove addiction pathways in our brains, but we can strengthen alternative ones. That means that if you are addicted to checking your phone, there is a pathway for that in your brain permanently, but you can pick up a new habit of playing the guitar or stretching your legs when you are bored instead.

When we're stressed out, it is easy to mispredict what will make us happy. It is almost always better to choose proactive habits than passive ones. It is really easy to think that watching TV after work or browsing through your phone for a couple of hours is a good idea. If we do something that requires some effort in the short-term, however, like going for a walk or meditating, we will often feel a lot better afterward. When we are stressed out, we shouldn't listen to our impulses. We must do what we know is right rather than what feels best right then and there. And we should change our habits sooner rather than later. Otherwise, it will be even harder to change them in the future.

GENERAL SUGGESTIONS TO AVOID DIGITAL DISTRACTION

Here are some practical ways you can take control of your digital life. Try the ones that resonate with you, and make a habit of the ones that require consistent action. If you do something enough times, you end up building a habit. Before you know it, practicing digital discipline will be effortless.

1. **Delete apps from your phone that distract you and move others into folders.**

   You will not have to expend as much self-control to avoid apps by removing potential distractions. Which apps do you open and get lost in? If you have apps you can't delete but want to use less, you can put them in folders so you can't instantly see them every time you open your phone.

2. **Turn off notifications.**
Many people receive hundreds of notifications daily from apps like Snapchat, Instagram, and Messenger. If you receive hundreds of Snaps a day and want to respond to them all, that cannot be done while having good digital habits. Being interrupted all day will hinder your productivity and reduce your presence. The best course of action is to adjust your notification settings so that unimportant apps don't disturb you. Instead, schedule time to check your phone so you avoid reacting to notifications every five minutes. Sound notifications are the most intrusive. You could also, for instance, turn off the sound on everything except calls. Turning off notifications can have some social consequences, but remember the most important aspect of quality time—it is done in person, not via digital messages.

3. **Access certain websites or platforms only from your computer.**
For example, you can create a rule that you can only use social networks on your laptop. This will create a bigger barrier to entry for wasting time on meaningless activities.

4. **Use AdBlock.**
Installing AdBlock on your browser allows you to avoid useless commercials or other kinds of distracting content.

5. **Call your friends.**
   Make a point of calling your friends rather than texting them. You will waste less time planning get-togethers and strengthen your bonds. Tell your friends that you are available for calls in specific parts of the day when you usually have extra time. Build a social circle where people engage with each other without checking their phones all the time. The friendships will get closer as well.

6. **Block certain websites.**
   Limit access to certain websites by blocking them. That can be very useful if they temporarily weaken your self-control. An excellent way to do this is to install Freedom, which enables you to lock yourself out for a chosen time to access only productive things. You can also install extensions to remove recommended videos from YouTube, for example.

7. **Design your environment in a clever way.**
   Make sure to construct your living space in a way that makes offline activities compelling. You can design a comfortable reading space that makes reading more relaxing and enjoyable.

8. **Buy an old Nokia phone for calling and texting only.**
   Many people choose to have one smartphone and one old-school phone. This way, you can be available for urgent matters when you only bring your old-school phone while ensuring you do not get distracted.

9. **Buy an alarm clock.**

   If you have an alarm clock, you will not have to use your smartphone when going to bed and waking up.

10. **Check in before you check your phone.**

    Do you have to check your phone to get updates on something important, or is it only your brain tricking you? Do a mental check-in that lasts at least thirty seconds before you check your phone. A lot of what we think is important at the moment turns out to be meaningless by just adding a brief pause. By delaying before we act on our impulses, we tend to spend less time surfing. In addition, if we make a habit of taking thirty seconds to pause, we become more present in our lives very quickly. Unless you have an important meeting, a meetup, or something else that requires checking your phone, try not to check it.

11. **Set targets for yourself throughout the day.**

    You can continually set goals for yourself throughout the day. For instance, most days, I do not look at my phone after 10:00 p.m. and often only take phone calls before 11:30 a.m. Sometimes it can be wise to set targets for avoiding digital use throughout the day based on how present we feel. If feelings of stress and anxiety arise, it can be wise not to look at anything online or check your phone for a few hours to regroup and get centered again. In these periods, you can work or do other things, but avoid using the internet for anything outside of what is strictly necessary for work. Setting targets throughout the day will ensure that you limit unconscious digital use. It will also strengthen your self-control.

12. **Wear a watch.**

If you have a watch, you do not have to check your phone every time you want to see what time it is. This will dramatically reduce the number of times you check your phone in a day.

13. **Schedule your day.**

Many people experience a lot of stress because they think they need to be available online constantly. We should have at least one period every day when we are unavailable. If you have some periods during the day when you are entirely free from interruptions, you will become much more relaxed. For instance, you could make a rule to never bring your phone or laptop into bed. Another great technique is to reserve at least half an hour of uninterrupted time after waking up. Most people reach for their cell phones immediately after waking up, which dictates the rest of their day. You can avoid checking your phone before going to bed as well.

14. **Take advantage of loss aversion.**

If you recall from chapter 3, we feel a greater emotional response when we lose something than when we win because of how our brains are wired. We can take advantage of loss aversion in many ways to make it easier to change our digital habits. Tell a friend that your screen time for a week will be within a specific limit; if you fail, you have to pay a fine. Most smartphones have a feature in the settings where you can see how much screen time you have spent daily and during the last week.

15. **Reward yourself for keeping going.**
Pat yourself on the back and reward yourself when you do well. To fully implement great digital habits, we need to condition our brains to feel doing so is worth it. If you want to do a digital detox for a day and pull it off, get yourself an ice cream or buy a new book! There is intrinsic motivation in practicing digital discipline. We tend to feel great when doing it, but it can nonetheless be wise to reward ourselves occasionally if we want to build new habits.

16. **Deal with temptation.**
Staying with the unpleasant feeling or temptation and simply accepting the discomfort is the key to overcoming compulsive behavior. If we accept the slight pain or discomfort that drives us to consume too much content passively, we are free to use the time differently.

17. **Put your phone in a different room when working.**
If you work from home or have another task that requires sustained attention, put your phone on silent and place it in a different room. Check it at predetermined times if you have to. This will increase your productivity and focus significantly.

18. **Find tech-free hobbies.**

Tech loses its grip on you if you spend time without it. After a weekend in the woods, you will have become much more accustomed to the subtle pace of life, and for a few days after, you will be less prone to check your phone compulsively. Build a lifestyle centered on activities that don't involve screens. This will remind you there is more to life, and it will be easier to cultivate digital discipline. Start doing activities like painting classes, hiking, playing football, playing board games, or whatever you find interesting that is tech-free!

19. **I encourage you to try the three-week challenge at the end of this chapter to cultivate digital discipline.**

WHAT IS DIGITAL DISCIPLINE?

What is digital discipline really? It is all about staying in the driver's seat of your digital habits and not being a passive spectator. It can mean logging on to social media, answering your friends' messages, and logging out immediately when you have done what you were supposed to do. It can be watching a specific video you had in mind and then leaving without watching anything else. It can involve answering emails and then going back to your life. Working and only researching things that directly align with your work is also a good example.

We should strive to minimize time spent passively consuming content after checking what we set out to do. At times, it can be worthwhile to explore new ideas and expand our horizons as a passive consumer, but we should proactively set a time for it.

Spending hours daily in passive mode is not a great way to use our time. In the end, everything comes down to whether you are in charge of your life or not. Are you proactively making decisions and figuring out the next step in your life, or have you left that control to mainstream media, your boss, your spouse, or someone else? Our digital habits are essentially a reflection of our real life habits. If we are passive consumers online, we tend to be passively engaged in our own lives as well. Therefore, a great step to taking control of your life is to control your digital habits consciously.

Digital discipline revolves around who and what controls your dopamine. Are you in charge, or is Silicon Valley in charge of your focus and actions? Do you set goals and plans and execute them, or do your smartphone apps give you highs and lows throughout the day? Disciplining our minds to use the internet proactively sounds easy, but it isn't easy in practice. If you want to use the internet proactively, you must build your self-control to a high level. There is no way around it. There will be periods when it is painful to develop your self-control, but in the end, it is all worth it. Then you can proactively use the fantastic resources available on the internet and avoid the pitfalls.

A way to measure our time online is to look for offline benefits. Do we use time online to support our offline lifestyle? If so, it might be time well spent if we are effective. On the other hand, if you spend a lot of time online on activities that give you very little offline, you waste your time. When we know deep down that our activities offer no real benefit, we will often feel guilty afterward. The key is to distinguish between online activities that benefit us and activities that only distract us.[96]

Deep down, you know which of your digital habits are positive or negative influences. Here are some things you can consider to become more aware of what kind of impact certain digital activities have on your life:

- How does it feel while doing the activity or after doing the activity?
- What kind of long-term consequences does it have?
- Is it aligned with your goals?
- Is this something you could proudly share with your friends, family, or coworkers?

We become more resistant to tech companies' efforts by taking daily breaks from digital consumption. Acclimating to the more subtle pleasures of real life by taking some hours off is the key to remaining in charge. Then the pull to continue consuming content will weaken. In addition, you will be more refreshed to work and handle the other challenges in your life when you take breaks from digital use.

Remember, the sensitivity of your dopamine system affects your happiness tremendously. That's why drug addicts feel so bad when they crave drugs—they have highly desensitized dopamine systems. As a result, they experience low dopamine levels when they aren't high. Restoring dopamine to healthy levels before taking drugs may dramatically improve overcoming addiction.[97] The addict will experience motivation outside of drugs again.

Likewise, to overcome compulsive behavior, we must go through a period where life seems dull and boring. When we get to the other side, we will have a greater capacity to enjoy life. In the attention economy, however, the big tech companies rely on desensitizing our dopamine circuits to carn rcvcnue; they are literally making us less happy. The key to living life to the fullest is to build enough mental strength to resist attempts at gaming our dopamine system.

LIFE'S SMALL PLEASURES

Ideally, you want to dive so deeply into tasks that you find fun in the small details. That will only happen if your brain is sensitized. Our environments are much more stimulating nowadays than they used to be, even just a few years ago. That is because we have added an extra layer of stimuli on top of what previous generations could have experienced with the intcrnct, TV, smartphones, movies, porn, and so on.

With a sensitized dopamine system, almost no problcm will seem impossible to solve, and adventure and possibilities will seem abundant. The cure for boredom is curiosity. We will only feel curious if our ncural circuits are sensitive enough to derive pleasure from simple things. We must break through the boredom and monotony to discover the hidden beauty right before our eyes.

INTERNET AND TECHNOLOGY ADDICTS ANONYMOUS

An excellent resource for people struggling with compulsive internet use is Internet and Technology Addicts Anonymous (ITAA). They host daily meetings where you can informally drop in for support and useful tips to overcome struggles.

ITAA has developed a clever system consisting of top lines, middle lines, and bottom lines to help you understand what digital uses are problematic for you. These are different for everyone, and you have to define them yourself. Doing that can be a very helpful tool for managing your digital use.

Top lines are activities that make us healthy and functional and improve how we feel about ourselves. These kinds of activities keep us happy, productive, and satisfied. They can be offline or beneficial uses of technology.

Middle lines are digital activities that trigger us. Personally, I want to avoid watching porn, and because scrolling on Instagram is a trigger for that, I should avoid it. For others, this can be simply checking their phones for no reason since that alone can pull them into spending too much time on social media. It is important to know our triggers so we can avoid our middle lines as much as possible.

Bottom lines are compulsive digital activities or addictions. We should avoid them at all costs. We get lost in these activities when we do them and cannot stop.[98]

You don't have to be addicted or have a compulsion. Defining what you don't want to spend time on online, what you should minimize, and what is okay or beneficial will help you become more disciplined. I encourage you to define your top, middle, and bottom lines. In addition, reflect on whether certain emotional states can trigger you to want to access bottom lines. We are all different, and for some people, certain social media apps, for example, can trigger them or cause compulsive behavior. Those apps should be avoided if that is the case.

Try to satisfy your emotional needs in places other than online! Build a life offline that fulfills you. It starts with avoiding your bottom lines and finding alternative ways to nurture your emotional needs.

THREE-WEEK CHALLENGE

Before taking this challenge, write down your top, middle, and bottom lines.

WEEK 1:

1. Abstain from bottom lines. You can still listen to music or watch YouTube videos, for instance, as long as they are not bottom lines.
2. Don't use any devices for half an hour after waking up and the last two hours before bedtime. This includes your TV, computer, and phone.
3. Only set notifications for messages and calls. Turn off all other notifications, and check social media apps only when you schedule time for it.

WEEK 2:

Continue doing everything from week one—most importantly, abstaining from bottom lines. In addition:

1. Don't use your devices when waiting in line, on the bus, during a rideshare, at a restaurant, or in typical moments of boredom during the day unless it is very important. You can still listen to music or watch a movie in the comfort of your home, but you need to adjust to having no digital stimuli outside your home. You can bring a book, for example, to kill time.

WEEK 3:

Continue doing everything from weeks one and two. In addition:

1. Abstain from all middle and bottom lines. It can be inconvenient to abstain from all potential triggers (middle lines) since common tools such as email can be a trigger for some, but be creative in finding workarounds.

2. Practice total digital discipline. Use the phone only when there is a good reason for it—no entertainment seeking. This means no movies, TV, music, or anything like it. You are only allowed to answer messages, calls, and emails and research things that are useful to you (only in written format). The point is to have a week with a sustainable digital detox, so you get used to relying on less stimuli in your daily life.

Habits are stacked every week because we can change only a few things at a time, and trying to implement too many things at once will make it very challenging. It is straightforward to change the notifications on your phone and stop using devices before bedtime and after waking up. Then, you can add a new habit every week.

Especially important is making a habit of not always checking the phone on the bus or while in line at Starbucks. Doing this will give you more pauses in your day and a lot more presence. I find that when I avoid checking the phone during small breaks, I get the chance to recharge between activities. If we always check the phone, we lose out on the possibility of calming down and relaxing fully.

DIGITAL DISCIPLINE: MAKE LASTING CHANGES

This challenge is meant to be a stretch, and you don't have to live like this for the rest of your life. But trying this will set you up to be a lot more disciplined with how you use your devices. If you fail, there is no point in beating yourself up. Simply write down at the end of the day where you had some missteps and why they happened, and offer a potential solution. Use that to do better the following day. If you manage to get through this challenge, I can assure you that you will feel more energetic and happier, and your productivity will increase tenfold. Most likely, you will start to feel that your relationships are getting better, and you will probably feel better physically and will naturally start being more active. Try it!

FINAL THOUGHTS

I t is challenging to notice something that changes gradually. But if you upgrade how you spend your time online and cut off scrolling after work every day, your life will improve over time. Massive change can occur when gradual change compounds over a year, but we don't really notice it from moment to moment. We are better at detecting sudden change than incremental change. How we engage with smartphones would seem entirely unreal for someone in the 2000s, yet everyone takes it for granted now. The small decisions we make at the moment might seem unimportant, but over time they stack up for better or worse.

Less is more when looking at news and staying updated. If we spend too much time online focused on the latest news and notifications, we lose the ability to tell what only distracts us and what contains factual information. Most of the content we are exposed to is only noise, and there are few bits of real information hidden in the noise.

There is a simple truth in life that all of us should accept: pain is inevitable. No matter what you do, you will experience some pain every day. When we are trying to change, we are only front-loading inevitable pain. You will have to face discomfort and gradually build your self-control until you are strong enough to allocate your time better. There is no other way around it. Doing this will make your life more pleasurable overall, and you will experience less pain throughout your lifetime.

You become stronger every time you encounter something uncomfortable. You also become more capable of living a life of your design when you overcome challenges. Become a mental athlete and view it as a competition with yourself: "Today, I will go a little longer than yesterday without checking my phone." You might set another challenge for yourself that has nothing to do with your phone. Exceeding your limitations produces a natural high. If you continue setting challenges and executing them, you will exceed what you thought was possible.

We spend time in two dimensions: the real world and the virtual one. The more time and energy we spend in the virtual one, the less effective we become in the real one. Apps have made us think about what to consume online rather than having real life experiences. Look around at people walking down the street. Few are present in the moment. Whenever we prioritize time with the people around us and avoid being passive online, we become more immersed in real life. Suddenly, you will exhibit childlike enthusiasm again and feel exhilarated.

And you will end up in a position where you can be a positive influence on others.

The key to living a happy and fulfilling life is to impose challenges on ourselves. When we remove the crutch of internet overuse, we are free to build a great life. The life you have always wanted is within reach. Good luck on your journey! Life is beautiful on the other side!

—Havard Mela

ACKNOWLEDGMENTS

I would like to thank everyone who helped make this book possible. It started with a gut feeling and the naivety to begin writing without any experience with publishers or literary agents. I wrote this book in the stillness of disconnecting from the distractions online. I am grateful for the support and encouraging words I received along the way from friends and family. Without their support, this book never would have come to life.

My friend Torgeir Klevstuen read through my first draft and gave me a lot of ideas on how to improve the writing. My main editor, Jenna Schrader-Love, did a fantastic job, and the book is indisputably better due to her efforts. She understood the idea at a deep level and went above and beyond. Christina Roth also did an incredible job and put some elegant touches on the project. Lastly, I am grateful to the publishing team at Morgan James, who has been very professional. I want to thank my author relations manager, Gayle West, who was very helpful throughout the process, and literary scout Isaiah Taylor, who believed in this book and helped me bring it to life!

ABOUT THE AUTHOR

Havard was born and raised in Norway. When he is not writing, he spends most of his time working as an engineer, reading, traveling, or playing sports. He is just a guy who loves to write and share insights from his path to living a better life.

Visit him online at www.havardmela.com.

PRACTICING DIGITAL DISCIPLINE

Hopefully, you found this book useful, and you are motivated and ready to be conscious of your digital habits. So what is next? Great opportunities await you if you put knowledge into practice. For more exercises and practical ways to cultivate digital discipline, claim your free bonus at www.havardmela.com/digital-discipline.

ENDNOTES

INTRODUCITON

1   Mark E. Czeisler et al., "Mental Health, Substance Use, and Suicidal Ideation during the COVID-19 Pandemic," *MMWR Morbidity and Mortality Weekly Report* 69, no. 32 (August 2020): 1049–57, https://dx.doi.org/10.15585/mmwr.mm6932a1external icon.

2   Jocko Willink and Leif Babin, *Extreme Ownership: How U.S. Navy Seals Lead and Win* (New York: St. Martin's Press, 2017).

3   "Daily Time Spent on Social Networking by Internet Users Worldwide from 2012 to 2022," Statista, August 22, 2022, https://www.statista.com/statistics/433871/daily-social-media-usage-worldwide/.

4 *Collins English Dictionary*, "self-discipline," accessed July 1, 2022, https://www.collinsdictionary.com/dictionary/english/self-discipline.

5 Harvey Mackay, "Discipline Is the Foundation for All Success," *Hartford Business Journal*, April 11, 2011, https://www.hartfordbusiness.com/article/discipline-is-the-foundation-for-all-success.

Chapter 1: Where Is Technology Taking Us?

6 Madeline Roache, "Facebook's Co-Founder Calls It a 'Powerful Monopoly' That Should Be Broken Up," *Time*, last modified May 9, 2019, https://time.com/5586559/facebook-chris-hughes-breakup-mark-zuckerberg/.

7 Parmy Olson, "WhatsApp Cofounder Brian Acton Gives the Inside Story on #DeleteFacebook and Why He Left $850 Million Behind," *Forbes*, September 26, 2018, https://www.forbes.com/sites/parmyolson/2018/09/26/exclusive-whatsapp-cofounder-brian-acton-gives-the-inside-story-on-deletefacebook-and-why-he-left-850-million-behind/?sh=6d6bee433f20.

8 Ezra Klein, "How Technology Is Designed to Bring Out the Worst in Us," *Vox*, February 19, 2018, https://www.vox.com/technology/2018/2/19/17020310/tristan-harris-facebook-twitter-humane-tech-time.

9 Tom Knowles, "Silicon Valley's Tech-Free Waldorf School Is a Hit," *The Times*, November, 10, 2018, https://www.thetimes.co.uk/article/silicon-valley-s-tech-free-school-is-a-hit-znqclhmg6.

10 Todd Love et al., "Neuroscience of Internet Pornography Addiction: A Review and Update," *Behavioral Sciences*

(Basel, Switzerland) 5, no. 3 (September 2015): 388–433, https://doi.org/10.3390/bs5030388.

11 N. D. Volkow et al., "Addiction: Decreased Reward Sensitivity and Increased Expectation Sensitivity Conspire to Overwhelm the Brain's Control Circuit," *BioEssays* 32, no. 9 (2010): 748–55, https://doi.org/10.1002/bies.201000042.

12 Love et al., "Neuroscience of Internet Pornography Addiction."

13 Mike Brooks, "The Seductive Pull of Screens That You Might Not Know About," *Psychology Today*, October 17, 2018, https://www.psychologytoday.com/us/blog/tech-happy-life/201810/the-seductive-pull-screens-you-might-not-know-about.

14 B. F. Skinner, "A Brief Survey of Operant Behaviour," B. F. Skinner Foundation, October 17, 2018, https://www.bfskinner.org/behavioral-science/definition/.

15 Cambridge Online Dictionary, "phubbing," accessed July 25, 2023, https://dictionary.cambridge.org/dictionary/english/phubbing.

16 David W. Moore, "Family, Health Most Important Aspects of Life: Money, Religion, Friends, and Work Roughly Equal in Importance," GALLUP, January 3, 2003, https://news.gallup.com/poll/7504/family-health-most-important-aspects-life.aspx.

17 Therese Fessenden, "The Principle of Commitment and Behavioral Consistency," Nielsen Norman Group, March 4, 2018, https://www.nngroup.com/articles/commitment-consistency-ux/.

18 Eckhart Tolle, *A New Earth: Awakening to Your Life's Purpose* (London: Penguin Life, 2005).

19 Asurion, "Americans Check Their Phones 96 Times a Day," November 21, 2019, https://www.asurion.com/press-releases/americans-check-their-phones-96-times-a-day/.

20 Jack Canfield with Janet Switzer, *The Success Principles: How to Get from Where You Are to Where You Want to Be* (New York: William Morrow, 2005), 189.

CHAPTER 2: STATISTICS ON TECHNOLOGY OVERUSE

21 "Daily Time Spent on Social Networking by Internet Users Worldwide from 2012 to 2022," Statista, August 22, 2022, https://www.statista.com/statistics/433871/daily-social-media-usage-worldwide/.

22 Kerry Allen, "China: Children Given Daily Time Limit on Douyin: Its Version of TikTok," BBC News, September 20, 2021, https://www.bbc.com/news/technology-58625934.

23 Kelly McSweeney, "This Is Your Brain on Instagram: Effects of Social Media on the Brain," Now, March 17, 2019, https://now.northropgrumman.com/this-is-your-brain-on-instagram-effects-of-social-media-on-the-brain/.

24 K. C. Madhav, Shardulendra Prasad Sherchand, and Samendra Sherchan, "Association between Screen Time and Depression among US Adults," *Preventive Medicine Reports* 8 (August 2017): 67–71, https://doi.org/10.1016/j.pmedr.2017.08.005.

25 Ethan Kross et al., "Facebook Use Predicts Declines in Subjective Well-Being in Young Adults," *PLoS ONE* 8, no. 8 (August 2013): e69841, https://doi.org/10.1371/journal.pone.0069841.

26 Seyyed Mohsen Azizi, Ali Soroush, and Alireza Khatony, "The Relationship between Social Networking Addiction and Academic Performance in Iranian Students of Medical Sciences: A Cross-Sectional Study," *BMC Psychology* 7, no. 1 (May 2019): 28, https://doi.org/10.1186/s40359-019-0305-0.

27 "Brain Drain: The Mere Presence of One's Own Smartphone Reduces Available Cognitive Capacity," *Journal of the Association for Consumer Research* 2, no. 2 (April 2017): 140–54, https://doi.org/10.1086/691462.

28 Mark Dolliver, "US Time Spent with Media 2019: Digital Time Keeps Rising as Growth Subsides for Total Time Spent," Insider Intelligence, May 30, 2019, https://www.insiderintelligence.com/content/us-time-spent-with-media-2019.

29 "Time Spent on Various Activities for Persons 16 74 Years. Average for All Days. Hours and Minutes," accessed July 25, 2022, *Statistics Norway*, https://www.ssb.no/204993/time-spent-on-various-activities-for-persons-16-74-years.average-for-all-days.hours-and-minutes-sy-16.

30 Nicole Lyn Pesce, "We Now Spend More Time on Netflix Than We Do Bonding with Our Kids," Market Watch, September 13, 2018, https://www.marketwatch.com/story/we-now-spend-more-time-on-netflix-than-we-do-bonding-with-our-kids-2018-09-13-12882032.

31 "New Report: Parents Spend More Than Nine Hours a Day with Screen Media," Common Sense Media, December 6, 2016, https://www.commonsensemedia.org/press-releases/new-report-parents-spend-more-than-nine-hours-a-day-with-screen-media.

32 "Loneliness and the Workplace: 2020 U.S. Report," Cigna, 2020, https://www.cigna.com/static/www-cigna-com/docs/about-us/newsroom/studies-and-reports/combatting-loneliness/cigna-2020-loneliness-report.pdf.

33 Amy Novotney, "The Risks of Social Isolation," *Monitor on Psychology* 50, no. 5 (May 2019), https://www.apa.org/monitor/2019/05/ce-corner-isolation.

34 Melissa G. Hunt, Rachel Marx, Courtney Lipson, and Jordyn Young, "No More FOMO: Limiting Social Media Decreases Loneliness and Depression," *Journal of Social and Clinical Psychology* 37, no. 10 (December 2018), https://doi.org/10.1521/jscp.2018.37.10.751.

35 Andrew K. Przybylski and Netta Weinstein, "Can You Connect with Me Now? How the Presence of Mobile Communication Technology Influences Face-to-Face Conversation Quality," *Journal of Social and Personal Relationships* 30, no. 3 (July 2012): 237–46. https://journals.sagepub.com/doi/full/10.1177/0265407512453827.

36 Shalini Misra, Lulu Cheng, Jamie Genevie, and Miao Yuan, "The iPhone Effect: The Quality of In-Person Social Interactions in the Presence of Mobile Devices," *Environment and Behavior* 48, no. 2 (February 2016): 275–98, https://www.researchgate.net/publication/270730343_The_iPhone_Effect_The_Quality_of_In-Person_Social_Interactions_in_the_Presence_of_Mobile_Devices.

37 A Mehrabian and S. R. Ferris, "Inference of Attitudes from Nonverbal Communication in Two Channels," *Journal of Consulting Psychology* 31, no. 3 (1967): 248–52, https://doi.org/10.1037/h0024648.

38 "Maarten W. Bos and Amy J. C. Cuddy, "iPosture: The Size of Electronic Consumer Devices Affects Our Behavior," Harvard Business School Working Paper 13-097 (Boston, MA: Harvard Business School, May 2013), https://www. hbs.edu/ris/Publication%20Files/13-097_4c473e46-e91b-4c9a-9070-ff61c7f70d3a.pdf.

39 Lone Frank, "Can Electrically Stimulating Your Brain Make You Too Happy?" *The Atlantic*, March 21, 2018, https://www.theatlantic.com/health/archive/2018/03/pleasure-shock-dccp-brain-stimulation-happiness/556043/.

40 Stephen Smith, "Radio: The Internet of the 1930s," American Public Media Reports, November 10, 2014, https://www.apmreports.org/episode/2014/11/10/radio-the-internet-of-the-1930s.

41 Vicki Wielenga and Dawna Gilchrist, "From Gold Medal Glory to Prohibition: The Early Evolution of Cocaine in the United Kingdom and the United States," *JRSM Short Reports* 4, no. 5 (April 2013): 2042533313478324, https://doi.org/10.1177/2042533313478324.

42 Hugh Levinson, "The Strange and Curious History of Lobotomy," *BBC News*, November 8, 2011, https://www.bbc.com/news/magazine-15629160.

43 David Comer Kidd and Emanuele Castano, "Reading Literary Fiction Improves Theory of Mind," *Science* 342, no. 6156 (October 2013): 377–80, https://doi.org/10.1126/science.1239918.

44 Michael Dambrun, "Self-Centeredness and Selflessness: Happiness Correlates and Mediating Psychological Pro-

cesses," *PeerJ* 2017, no. 5 (June 2017): e3306, https://doi.org/10.7717/peerj.3306.

CHAPTER 3: HOW DOES THE BRAIN WORK?

45 Elizabeth A. Weaver II and Hilary H. Doyle, "How Does the Brain Work?" Dana Foundation, August 11, 2019, https://www.dana.org/article/how-does-the-brain-work/.

46 Frederico A. C. Azevedo et al., "Equal Numbers of Neuronal and Nonneuronal Cells Make the Human Brain an Isometrically Scaled-Up Primate Brain," *Journal of Comparative Neurology* 513, no. 5 (February 2009): 532–41, https://doi.org/10.1002/cne.21974.

47 Alberto Del Arco and Francisco Mora, "Prefrontal Cortex–Nucleus Accumbens Interaction: In Vivo Modulation by Dopamine and Glutamate in the Prefrontal Cortex," *Pharmacology, Biochemistry, and Behavior* 90, no. 2 (August 2008): 226–35, https://doi.org/10.1016/j.pbb.2008.04.011.

48 Alex Korb, *The Upward Spiral: Using Neuroscience to Reverse the Course of Depression, One Small Change at a Time* (Oakland, CA: New Harbinger Publications, 2015), 72.

49 Korb, The Upward Spiral, 5.

50 William D. S. Killgore, Elizabeth A. Olson, and Mareen Weber, "Physical Exercise Habits Correlate with Gray Matter Volume of the Hippocampus in Healthy Adult Humans," *Scientific Reports* 3, no. 3457 (2013), https://doi.org/10.1038/srep03457.

51 Kendra Cherry, "What Is Neuroplasticity?" Verywell Mind, last modified November 8, 2022, https://www.verywellmind.com/what-is-brain-plasticity-2794886.

52 Hejab Maazer Alfawareh and Shaidah Jusoh, "The Use and Effects of Smartphones in Higher Education," *International Journal of Interactivities Mobile Technologies* 11, no. 6 (November 2017): 103–11, https://doi.org/10.3991/ijim.v11i6.7453.

53 G. J. Madden, N. M. Petry, G. J. Badger, and W. K. Bickel, "Impulsive and Self-Control Choices in Opioid-Dependent Patients and Non-Drug-Using Control Patients: Drug and Monetary Rewards," *Experimental and Clinical Psychopharmacology* 5, no. 3 (1997): 256–62, https://doi.org/10.1037/1064-1297.5.3.256.

CHAPTER 4: HOW TECHNOLOGY EXPLOITS US

54 Susan Weinschenk, "Use Unpredictable Rewards to Keep Behavior Going," *Psychology Today*, November 13, 2013, https://www.psychologytoday.com/us/blog/brainwise/201311/use-unpredictable-rewards-keep-behavior-going.

55 Mike Snyder, "Netflix's Biggest Competition? Sleep, CEO Says," *USA Today*, April 18, 2017, https://eu.usatoday.com/story/tech/talkingtech/2017/04/18/netflixs-biggest-compctition-sleep-ceo-says/100585788/.

56 Charlie Munger, "The Psychology of Human Misjudgment" (speech, Harvard University, Boston, MA, 1995), JamesClear.com, https://jamesclear.com/great-speeches/psychology-of-human-misjudgment-by-charlie-munger.

57 Troels W. Kjaer et al., "Increased Dopamine Tone during Meditation-Induced Change of Consciousness," *Cognitive Brain Research* 13, no. 2 (April 2002): 255–9, https://doi.org/10.1016/S0926-6410(01)00106-9.

58 N. D. Volkow et al., "Addiction: Decreased Reward Sen-
    sitivity and Increased Expectation Sensitivity Conspire to
    Overwhelm the Brain's Control Circuit," *BioEssays* 32, no.
    9 (2010): 748–55, https//:doi.org/10.1002/bies.201000042.

59 Andrew Huberman, 23. September 2021. "Dopamine
    Detox: Take Back Control of Your Life and Stop Laziness!"
    Tom Bilyeu, September 23, 2021, YouTube video, https://
    www.youtube.com/watch?v=xLORsLlcT48.

60 Rich McCormick, "Odds Are We're Living in a Simulation,
    Says Elon Musk," The Verge, June 2, 2016, https://www.
    theverge.com/2016/6/2/11837874/elon-musk-says-odds-
    living-in-simulation.

61 M. Arain, M. Haque, L. Johal, P. Mathur, W. Nel, A. Rais,
    R. Sandhu, and S. Sharma, "Maturation of the Adolescent
    Brain," *Neuropsychiatric Disease and Treatment* 9 (April
    2013): 449–61, https://doi.org/10.2147/NDT.S39776.

62 Matthew Hutson, "People Prefer Electric Shocks to Being
    Alone with Their Thoughts," *The Atlantic*, July 3, 2014,
    https://www.theatlantic.com/health/archive/2014/07/
    people-prefer-electric-shocks-to-being-alone-with-their-
    thoughts/373936/.

63 Soyeon Kim et al., "Differential Associations between
    Passive and Active Forms of Screen Time and Adolescent
    Mood and Anxiety Disorders," *Social Psychiatry and Psy-
    chiatric Epidemiology* 55, no. 11 (February 2020): 1469–
    78, https://doi.org/10.1007/s00127-020-01833-9.

CHAPTER 5: WHAT MAKES US HAPPY?

64 Jean M. Twenge, "The Sad State of Happiness in the United States and the Role of Digital Media," World Happiness Report, March 20, 2019, https://worldhappiness.report/ed/2019/the-sad-state-of-happiness-in-the-united-states-and-the-role-of-digital-media/.

65 Jean M. Twenge and W. Keith Campbell, "Associations between Screen Time and Lower Psychological Well-Being among Children and Adolescents: Evidence from a Population-Based Study," *Preventive Medicine Reports* 12 (December 2018): 271–83, https://doi.org/10.1016/j.pmedr.2018.10.003.

66 Scott Barry Kaufman, "The Differences between Happiness and Meaning in Life," *Scientific American,* January 30, 2016, https://blogs.scientificamerican.com/beautiful-minds/the-differences-between-happiness-and-meaning-in-life/.

67 Philip Strandwitz, "Neurotransmitter Modulation by the Gut Microbiota," *Brain Research* 1693, Pt B (August 2018): 128–33, https://doi.org/10.1016/j.brainres.2018.03.015.

68 A. Marotta, E. Sarno, A. Del Casale, M. Pane, L. Mogna, A. Amoruso, G. E. Felis, and M. Fiorio, "Effects of Probiotics on Cognitive Reactivity, Mood, and Sleep Quality," *Frontiers in Psychiatry* 10 (March 2019): 164, https://doi.org/10.3389/fpsyt.2019.00164.

69 Linda Roszak Burton, "The Neuroscience of Gratitude: What You Need to Know about the New Neural Knowledge," October 2016, Wharton Health Care Management

Alumni Association, https://www.whartonhealthcare.org/ the_neuroscience_of_gratitude.

70 Leslie J. Seltzer, Ashley R. Prososki, Toni E. Ziegler, and Seth D. Pollak, "Instant Messages vs. Speech: Hormones and Why We Still Need to Hear Each Other," *Evolution and Human Behavior* 33, no. 1 (January 2012): 42–5, https:// doi.org/10.1016/j.evolhumbehav.2011.05.004.

71 Ibid.

72 Birgitta Dresp-Langley, "Children's Health in the Digital Age," *International Journal of Environmental Research and Public Health* 17, no. 9 (May 6, 2020): 3240, https:// doi.org/10.3390/ijerph17093240.

73 Genevieve Rayner, "The Emotion Centre Is the Oldest Part of the Human Brain: Why Is Mood So Important?" The Conversation, September 25, 2016, https://theconversation. com/the-emotion-centre-is-the-oldest-part-of-the-human-brain-why-is-mood-so-important-63324.

74 Kostadin Kushlev and Elizabeth W. Dunn, "Smartphones Distract Parents from Cultivating Feelings of Connection When Spending Time with Their Children," *Journal of Social and Personal Relationships* 36, no. 6 (April 2018): 1619–39, https://doi.org/10.1177/0265407518769387.

75 N. Epley and J. Schroeder, "Mistakenly Seeking Solitude," Journal of Experimental Psychology: General 143, no. 5 (2014): 1980–999, https://doi.org/10.1037/a0037323.

76 John D. Rockefeller Quotes, Brainy Quote, accessed July 25, 2023, https://www.brainyquote.com/quotes/john_d_ rockefeller_147467.

CHAPTER 6: THE KEYS TO HABIT CHANGE

77 Jocko Willink and Leif Babin, Extreme Ownership: How U.S. Navy Seals Lead and Win (New York, NY: St. Martin's Press, 2017).

78 Lucius Annaeus Seneca, *On the Shortness of Life*, trans. C. D. N. Costa (New York: Penguin Books, 1997).

79 Brendon Burchard's official website, accessed February 2, 2022, https://brendon.com.

80 George Orwell, *1984* (New York: Signet Classic, 1961).

81 Aldous Huxley, *Brave New World* (London: Chatto & Windus, 1932).

CHAPTER 7: FINDING PURPOSE

82 Mark Murphy, "Neuroscience Explains Why You Need to Write Down Your Goals If You Actually Want to Achieve Them," *Forbes*, April 15, 2018, https://www.forbes.com/sites/markmurphy/2018/04/15/neuroscience-explains-why-you-need-to-write-down-your-goals-if-you-actually-want-to-achieve-them/?sh=7d9d40279059.

83 Viktor E. Frankl, *Man's Search for Meaning* (Boston: Beacon Press, 2006).

84 David Deida, *The Way of the Superior Man: A Spiritual Guide to Mastering the Challenges of Women, Work, and Sexual Desire* (Boulder, CO: Sounds True, 2017).

85 Justin Bariso, "Warren Buffett's 25/5 Rule Will Help You Learn to Set Priorities, Achieve Focus, and Advance Your Career," Thrive Global, November 1, 2019, https://thrive-global.com/stories/need-to-set-priorities-achieve-

focus-and-advance-your-career-following-warren-buffetts-25-5-can-help/.

CHAPTER 8: HOW TO BUILD SELF-CONTROL

86 "Sir Ernest Shackleton Endurance Expedition: Trans-Antarctica 1914–1917," Cool Antarctica, accessed July 25, 2023, https://www.coolantarctica.com/Antarctica%20 fact%20file/History/Shackleton-Endurance-Trans-Antarctic_expedition.php.

87 Hakan Turkcapar, Samet Kose, Ahmet Ince, and Hugh Myrick, "Beliefs as a Predictor of Relapse in Alcohol-Dependent Turkish Men," *Journal of Studies on Alcohol* 66, no. 6 (November 2005): 848–51, https://doi.org/10.15288/jsa.2005.66.848.

88 David Goggins, *Can't Hurt Me: Master Your Mind and Defy the Odds* (Austin, TX: Lioncrest Publishing, 2018).

89 Didrik Espeland, Louis de Weerd, and James B. Mercer, "Health Effects of Voluntary Exposure to Cold Water – a Continuing Subject of Debate," *International Journal of Circumpolar Health* 81, no. 1 (September 2022): 2111789, https://doi.org/10.1080/22423982.2022.2111789.

CHAPTER 9: REBUILDING YOUR ABILITY TO FOCUS

90 Heather A. Wadlinger and Derek M. Isaacowitz, "Fixing Our Focus: Training Attention to Regulate Emotion," *Personality and Social Psychology Review* 15, no. 1 (February 2011): 75–102, https://doi.org/10.1177/1088868310365565.

91 A. Westbrook et al., "Dopamine Promotes Cognitive Effort by Biasing the Benefits Versus Costs of Cognitive Work,"

Science 367, no. 6484 (2020): 1362–366, https://doi. org/10.1126/science.aaz5891.

92 Éilish Duke and Christian Montag, "Smartphone Addiction, Daily Interruptions and Self-Reported Productivity," *Addictive Behaviors Reports* 6 (July 2017): 90–95, https:// doi.org/10.1016/j.abrep.2017.07.002.

93 Tim Ferris, "Bill Clinton Has a Superpower, and Mastering It Can Make You Successful Beyond Belief," *Huffington Post*, August 8, 2013, https://www.huffpost.com/entry/ bill-clinton_n_3718956.

94 Matthew A. Killingsworth and Daniel T. Gilbert, "A Wandering Mind Is an Unhappy Mind," *Science* 330, no. 6006 (2010): 932, https://doi.org/10.1126/science.1192439.

95 Terrell Heick, "Bloom's Taxonomy Is a Hierarchical Framework for Cognition and Learning Objectives," TeachThought University, August 14, 2018, https://www. teachthought.com/learning/what-is-blooms-taxonomy/.

CHAPTER 10: DIGITAL DISCIPLINE: MAKE LASTING CHANGES

96 Kostadin Kushlev and Elizabeth W. Dunn, "Smartphones Distract Parents from Cultivating Feelings of Connection When Spending Time with Their Children," *Journal of Social and Personal Relationships* 36, no. 6 (April 2018): 1619–39, https://doi.org/10.1177/0265407518769387.

97 Marco Diana, "The Dopamine Hypothesis of Drug Addiction and Its Potential Therapeutic Value," *Front Psychiatry* 2, no. 64 (November 2011), https://doi.org/10.3389/ fpsyt.2011.00064.

98 "Tools of Recovery," Internet and Technology Addicts Anonymous, last modified March 27, 2023, https:// internetaddictsanonymous.org/resources/tools-of-recovery/.

A free ebook edition is available with the purchase of this book.

To claim your free ebook edition:

1. Visit MorganJamesBOGO.com
2. Sign your name CLEARLY in the space
3. Complete the form and submit a photo of the entire copyright page
4. You or your friend can download the ebook to your preferred device

Morgan James
BOGO™

A **FREE** ebook edition is available for you
or a friend with the purchase of this print book.

CLEARLY SIGN YOUR NAME ABOVE

Instructions to claim your free ebook edition:
1. Visit MorganJamesBOGO.com
2. Sign your name CLEARLY in the space above
3. Complete the form and submit a photo
   of this entire page
4. You or your friend can download the ebook
   to your preferred device

Print & Digital Together Forever.

Snap a photo

Free ebook

Read anywhere